U.S. Highway 89

The Scenic Route to Seven Western National Parks

Text and Photographs by Ann Torrence

U.S. Highway 89

The Scenic Route to Seven Western National Parks

Text and Photographs by Ann Torrence

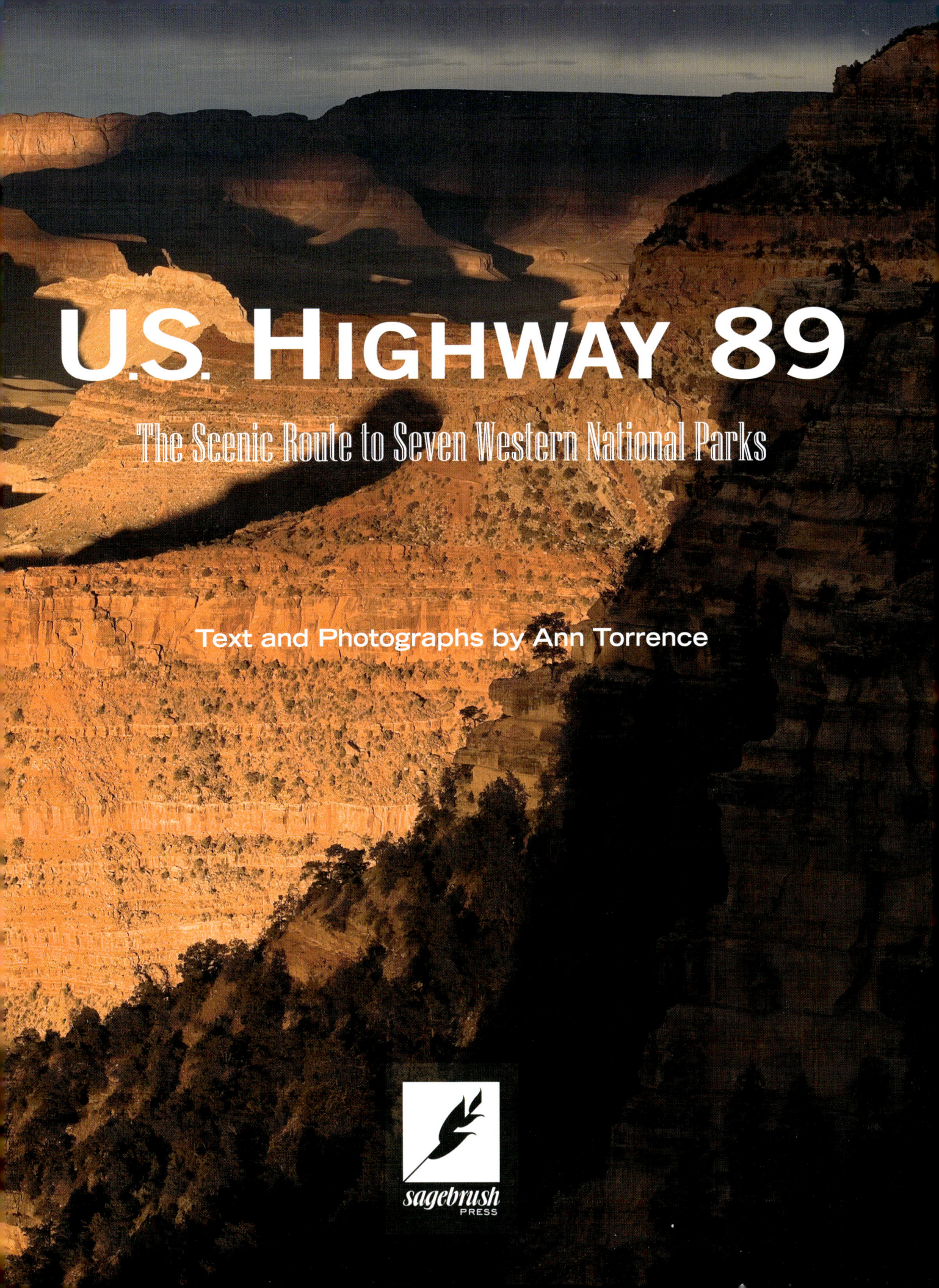

sagebrush PRESS

★ ★ ★ Acknowledgements ★ ★ ★ ★ ★ ★ ★ ★ ★ ★ ★

For their support and advice early in the project: Robert Dick, Patricia Goede, Nancy Green, Bryan Jones, Marlene Lambert, Dawn Marano, Zeke McCabe, Gary Topping, and Monte Bona, Utah Heritage Highway 89 Alliance; for assistance in research and access to photographic locations: Wade and Tina Eliason; President Dean Halling, Mormon Miracle Pageant; Richard Justis, Logan Scenic Byway Commission; Mike Milne and the Customs and Border Protection officers at the Piegan Port of Entry; Robert Newkirk; Harley and Diane Pebley; Bert Raynes; Mary Scriver; Becky Smith, National Oregon/California Trail Center; Tucson International Mariachi Conference; Tony Varilone, Oregon Trail-Bear Lake Scenic Byway Committee; Jane Weber, Lewis & Clark Interpretive Center. Thank you to Jennie Garramon for leading me to the *Choteau Acantha* archives; Wayne Johnson for background on Grand Teton National Park and the river-running on the Snake River; Joe and Phyllis Greene and Bert Raynes for behind-the-scenes views of Jackson's nesting boxes; Reed Thomas and Dean Barney. For taking me aloft for aerial photography: Clark Fogle, Adriel Heisey, Maria Langer. For invitations to present my Highway 89 work: Bruce Hucko, Moab Photo Symposium; Ross Walker, Bear Lake Photography Seminar; Jesse Harding, Ignite Salt Lake. Greta DeJong and Dr. Paul Gahlinger made it possible to publish through Sagebrush Press. Pam Fogle, Rich Legg and Charles Uibel provided essential editing of words and photographs. Michael Smith, for my home-away-from-home in Phoenix. My husband, Robert Marc, traveled border-to-border with me on Highway 89, read my first drafts, made the maps and is my biggest fan.

★ ★ ★ ★ ★ ★ ★ ★ ★ ★ ★ ★ ★ ★ ★ ★ ★ ★ ★ ★

Sagebrush Press

Copyright © 2009 Ann Torrence
All rights reserved. No part of this book may be reproduced in any form without written permission from the publisher.

Published by Sagebrush Press
Salt Lake City, Utah 84105

ISBN 978-0-9703130-5-8
Library of Congress Control Number: 2009907269

Printed in Korea.
First Printing, Summer 2009

Contents

See America First   7
Mexico to Canada

In Father Kino's Footsteps   15
Nogales to Tucson, Arizona

Arizona's First Highway   27
Tucson to Route 66, Arizona

The Honeymoon Trail   45
Flagstaff to Page, Arizona

Mormon Heritage Highway   65
Big Water to Thistle, Utah

The Wasatch Front   85
Spanish Fork to Garden City, Utah

Riding with the Committee   105
Fish Haven to Geneva, Idaho

Greater Yellowstone   113
Star Valley, Wyoming, to Yellowstone National Park

The Park-to-Park Highway   131
Gardiner to Piegan, Montana

Epilogue   153
The Character of the American West

Index   156

Resources for Travelers   158

THE BIG CUT: Highway 89 was rerouted through the "Big Cut" near Page, Arizona, a 300' deep excavation through the Echo Cliffs, after the 1957 opening of the Glen Canyon Bridge over the Colorado River. (above)

HIGHWAY 89: northern Montana (page 1)

YAVAPAI POINT: Grand Canyon National Park (pages 2–3)

US Highway 89 ★ 5

89 Driving U.S 89 today

U.S. Highway 89 has had three major configurations in its first 80 years: the 1926 route from Nogales, Arizona, to Spanish Fork, Utah; the 1938 extension from to Piegan, Montana; and after the Arizona section from Nogales was decommissioned in 1992, the highway ran from Flagstaff, Arizona, to Piegan.

Other realignments occurred as new interstate freeways overlaid sections of U.S. 89: from Nogales to Tucson, around Utah's Wasatch Front and in Great Falls, Montana. For the most part, this book follows the 1955 route, the year before interstate freeway construction began.

After decommissioning, much of U.S. 89 was simply renumbered as Arizona state highways. Originally, the highway began at the Nogales border crossing and went northward along Grand Avenue, becoming the Tucson-Nogales Highway. Today's motorists join Interstate 19 leaving Nogales, as the frontage road is no longer continuous in Santa Cruz County. At exit 69 (I-19 is marked in kilometers) take Business I-19 northward, which becomes 6th Avenue in Tucson.

North from Tucson's center, 6th Avenue becomes Oracle Road (Arizona 77). At Oracle Junction, turn left onto Arizona 79 to Florence Junction. Turn left when Arizona 79 ends at the intersection with U.S. 60. Highway 89 used to merge with U.S. 60, which has since become a major east-west freeway serving the Phoenix metroplex. Instead, at Apache Junction, exit U.S 60 and take Apache Trail west. As it enters Mesa, it becomes Main Street. In Tempe, continue on Main Street to Mill Avenue, and cross the Mill Avenue Bridge over the Salt River.

Entering Phoenix, the road changes names to Van Buren Street. Continue west on Van Buren through downtown Phoenix. At Grand Avenue, turn right (northwest), eventually rejoining U.S. 60 all the way to Wickenburg.

The old Highway 89 splits from U.S. 60 in the heart of Wickenburg. Turn right onto U.S. 93, and in 4.5 miles, right onto Arizona 89. Follow Arizona 89 all the way from Wickenburg to Ashfork. In Ashfork, U.S. 89 merged with Route 66 to Flagstaff. Short sections of Route 66 are drivable, particularly around Williams, but Interstate 40 is the direct route. On the east side of Flagstaff, an exit from I-40 marks the official beginning of today's U.S. 89.

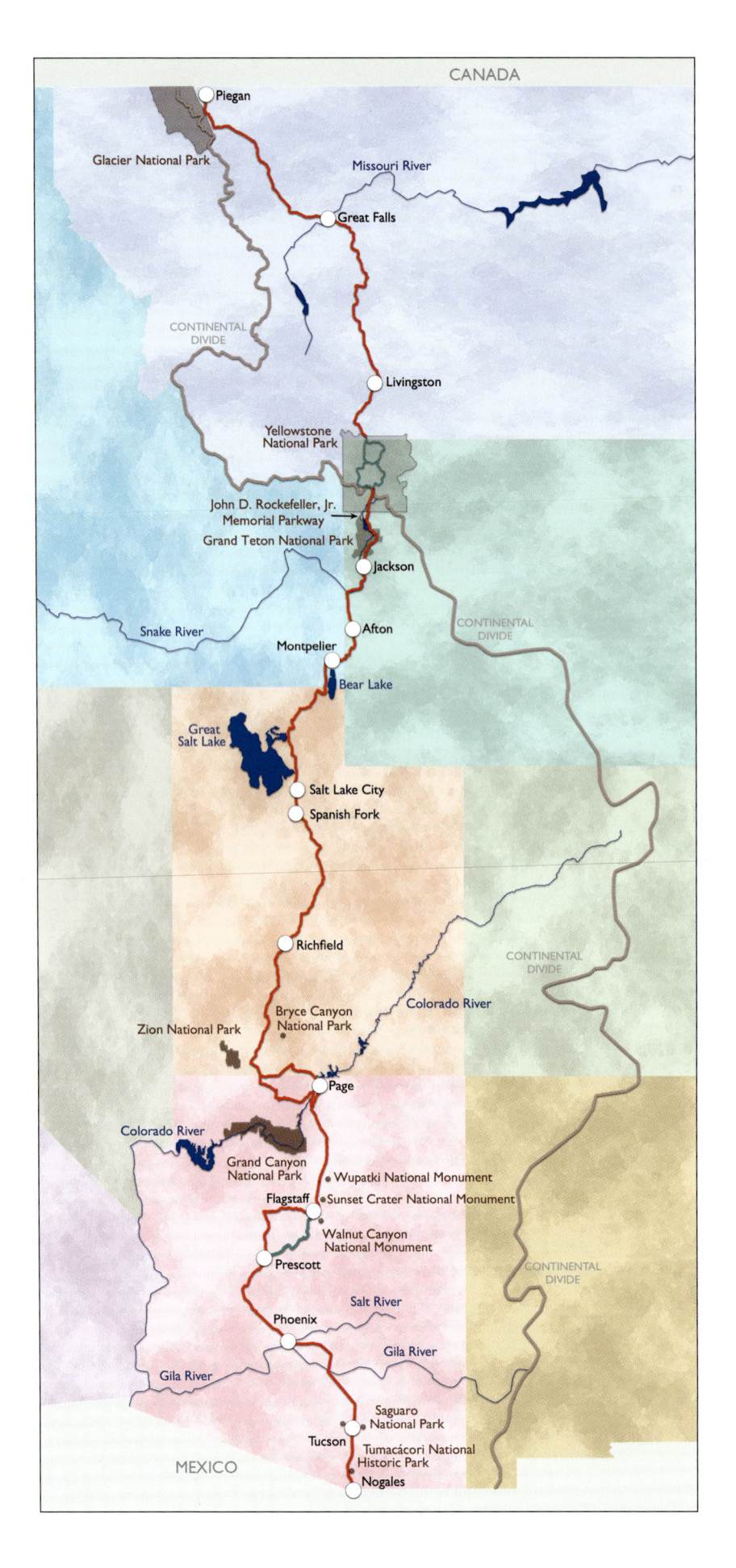

6 ★ US Highway 89

See America First
★ ★ ★ Mexico to Canada ★ ★ ★ ★ ★ ★ ★ ★ ★ ★

The great American road trip demands an automobile, a highway and a destination. This book tells the story of U.S. Highway 89, part of the country's first national highway system, the spectacular treasures in its seven national parks, the people and communities along the way, and how they came to share this magnificent highway.

U.S. 89 was mapped out as part of the nation's first federal highway system in 1926. Thomas MacDonald, chief of the Bureau of Public Roads (BPR), had an ambitious goal: to link together every county courthouse in America with a paved road rated for 35 mph travel. Sections of the numbered routes simply replaced and improved existing named highways, like the Lincoln Highway, which became much of U.S. 40. But for long stretches in the rural West, the federal highways finally lifted America's automobile rims out of the mud.

The fact that Highway 89 linked seven national parks is a happy accident of geography. When the federal highway map was proposed, Yellowstone National Park was more than 50 years old, but Glacier had only celebrated its 15-year anniversary. Zion and Grand Canyon had just come into the National Park Service. Bryce Canyon, Grand Teton and Saguaro national parks did not exist. BPR planners designed a network of highways, and the parks simply aligned on the same north-south corridor. The highway curves around natural obstacles, like the Great Salt Lake, and crosses some challenging terrain, like the Continental Divide and the Colorado River, but for the most part, U.S. 89 was one strand of a system that wove rural America into a nationwide grid.

PARRY LODGE: In the 1920s, the Parry Brothers offered auto tours of the Grand Circle: today's Bryce Canyon, Zion and North Rim of Grand Canyon National Parks. They expanded into lodging (above) in 1931 to host the increasing number of film crews working in the Kanab area.

Motoring across America
Widespread adoption of the automobile transformed American culture in less than a generation and, by the 1920s, motoring made tourism affordable for a growing middle class. Motorists invented

TUCSON INTERNATIONAL MARIACHI CONFERENCE: 1000 students participate each year in the Tucson International Mariachi Conference, learning from and then performing with maestros from the U.S. and Mexico. The musicians' charro costume is rooted in Jalisco cowboy and rodeo tradition. (above)

AUTUMN IN ZION NATIONAL PARK: Cottonwood trees line the Big Bend of the Virgin River below Angel's Landing. (right)

the road trip vacation: average citizens hit the road, camping gear strapped to the running boards, and they headed to their national parks. The roads were deplorable.

In 1915, for the first time, the number of horse-drawn vehicles manufactured in the United States was equalled by automobile production. Road-building, traditionally a county responsibility and often relegated to convict labor, lagged far behind. An unsurfaced track to the nearest railhead was perhaps sufficient for farmer and wagon, but the new motorists demanded roads with wider lanes, curves engineered for faster, safer turns and all-weather surfaces. Most importantly, they wanted highways for long-distance travel.

How to rebuild the nation's muddy wagon ruts for automobiles? Who would pay for it? Should the counties or states expand their public services, or was this a new role for the federal government? Debating these questions occupied legislative bodies for years, while actual progress was slow and uncoordinated across state lines.

Leaders of local commercial clubs, anxious to steer profitable traffic through their towns, and motorists, formed dozens of "Good Roads" committees and highway associations. These groups published booklets and maps, organized rallies and races, advocated for public road-building, and in some cases actually built roads themselves. The Yellowstone Trail, Pikes Peak Ocean-to-Ocean Highway and Park-to-Park Highway, all long-distance roads heavily promoted to tourists, resulted from these volunteer road-building programs.

Each highway association chose colors and symbols to mark its route. Good Roads promoter William Rishel explained the unintended results in Utah: "Salt Lake City was perhaps blessed, or should I say cursed, with more highway associations than any other city in America. At one time, there were no less than 14 highway and trail associations claiming State Street as their own particular route. The telephone and light poles looked like barber signposts with the associations' different identification bands painted in different colors."

Both the Bureau of Public Roads (BPR) and the National Park Service were created in 1916, but resources were increasingly directed toward an inevitable American role in World War I. After the war, road-building supplies and equipment were repatriated for domestic highway construction. The federal government distributed not only heavy equipment but vast quantities of hand tools, like picks and shovels, to the states. The Bureau of Public Roads' first attempts at a federal-state road-building partnership ran into roadblocks—some states did not have a highway department in place to accept federal funding. Worse, matching funds often built city and regional roads. The states' lack of interstate cooperation ranged from frustrating to

SWIFTCURRENT CREEK: Glacier National Park

ridiculous: some federally funded roads simply did not join at state borders.

In 1921, the BPR developed a new strategy: states could only get matching highway funds if they first created a state highway department to manage the grants. The states then had to nominate no more than seven percent of their state's mileage to form an interstate highway network. The BPR delegated to the American Association of State Highway Officials the task (and political woes of dealing with local officials campaigning for primary routes through their towns) of mapping a unified proposal for a federal primary highway system. With the military's input, in 1926, the BPR finalized the routes and numbering system that officially created U.S. Highway 89.

Parks for the People
During World War I, the slogan "See America First" inspired many Americans to visit the western United States as a substitute for a "grand tour" of Europe. Stephen Mather and his staff in the Department of the Interior did not invent the phrase, but skillfully co-opted it to promote national park tourism. Mather, a 47-year-old mining millionaire, entered public service to transform some 20 national parks and monuments scattered in three cabinet-level departments (Agriculture, War and Interior) into a cohesive agency. His deputy, Horace Albright, a California law student, had mastered the intricacies of Washington politics, and between them they ushered through the legislation to create the National Park Service in 1916.

Public relations campaigns brought in droves of tourists, and by 1920, the majority of national park visitors reached their destinations by automobile. The parks' roads, if they existed at all, were generally inadequate for the increased traffic. Mather formed a partnership with the Bureau of Public Roads to provide expertise for numerous road-building projects undertaken in the parks in the 1920s.

Building the parks' infrastructure introduced a new challenge: how to build roads across the landscape while protecting its scenic beauty. Mather and Albright established a landscape division specifically to ensure that roads blended harmoniously into the terrain. The National Park Service invented unprecedented standards for road construction, specifying that native stone be used for bridgework, road alignments be contoured to the terrain, and vegetation be restored at the end of a project. Two of the largest projects became signature features of the parks themselves: the Zion–Mt. Carmel Tunnel in Zion National Park and Glacier's Going-to-the-Sun Road, both of which join Highway 89.

Roads to the parks often needed more work than those within NPS boundaries. Mather supported various "good roads" associations, attending their meetings and hosting their pathfinding tours, like the

89 Volunteer road-building

With only two weeks to get the road in shape before the Yellowstone Hotel & Transportation Co. began operating its stage car routes, the May 1, 1919, issue of the *Choteau Acantha* reported that "the residents of Browning set aside two afternoons of the present week for volunteer road work." The paper noted that 10 cars per day were scheduled to travel the highway between Yellowstone and Glacier National Park, stopping for lunch in Choteau. The report added that more volunteers from Choteau might be needed to clear rocks from the road.

89 A new motor tourist rush

"A great north and south highway from Canada to South America! That is the destiny of U.S. 89," extolled Ray Vyne, the Yavapai County Immigration Commissioner in his 1936 pamphlet addressed to tourists and potential residents.

Asserting that Highway 89 was about to become the backbone of the Pan-American Highway, he declared, "There is probably not another traffic route in the western states which presents to many scenes of natural grandeur. A new motor tourist rush has begun over a new, romantic trail which gradually will push farther and farther afield until it reaches all of the countries of the Western Hemisphere, from the Arctic Circle in the north to the Antarctic in the south — and Arizona is the hub and gateway."

Park-to-Park Highway Association's 1916 visit to Yellowstone. Not everyone was convinced of the economic benefits to improving tourist access. In 1917, Utah's German-born governor, Simon Bamberger, shouted down Albright's request to improve access to the future Zion National Park with, "I build no more roads to rocks!" Federal aid programs eventually helped finance park access roads; tourism dollars transformed rural economies, and government travel councils still promote "their" highways as the best routes to neighboring parks.

Romance of the Road

Route 66 has a song, the Lincoln Highway has a statue of the president himself at the Continental Divide. Over the years, the country's east-west routes have monopolized the romance of the road. Lacking a trademark or slogan, Highway 89 has been overlooked and under-appreciated by both tourists and locals, who tend to think of it as "their" road to the next big town. Yet, after a century at the wheel, the road trip to America's national parks has lost none of its appeal. For millions of motorists and their families, the parks are the quintessential road trip destination, and Highway 89 is the route to some of the most well-loved and frequently visited national parks.

From border to border and park to park, less than 300 miles of Highway 89's historic 1,600-mile route has been overlaid by interstate freeways. Today's hurried vacationers may not have time to drive U.S. 89 from Mexico to Canada, but shorter sojourns offer plenty of road trip delights. Mom-and-pop cafes still serve home-made pie, a cattle-drive may slow traffic to a crawl, and a homecoming parade can grind it to a halt.

On U.S. 89, visitors can experience both the jewels of the national parks and the slow route to a western America that is hanging onto its traditions while making its way into the 21st century. As the road trip of a lifetime, or by taking a lifetime to explore its hidden secrets, driving Highway 89 is one of America's most scenic and pleasurable adventures.

MONSOON SEASON: Saguaro National Park (opposite)

CRUISING: Riding on historic Highway 89 south of Florence, Arizona (above)

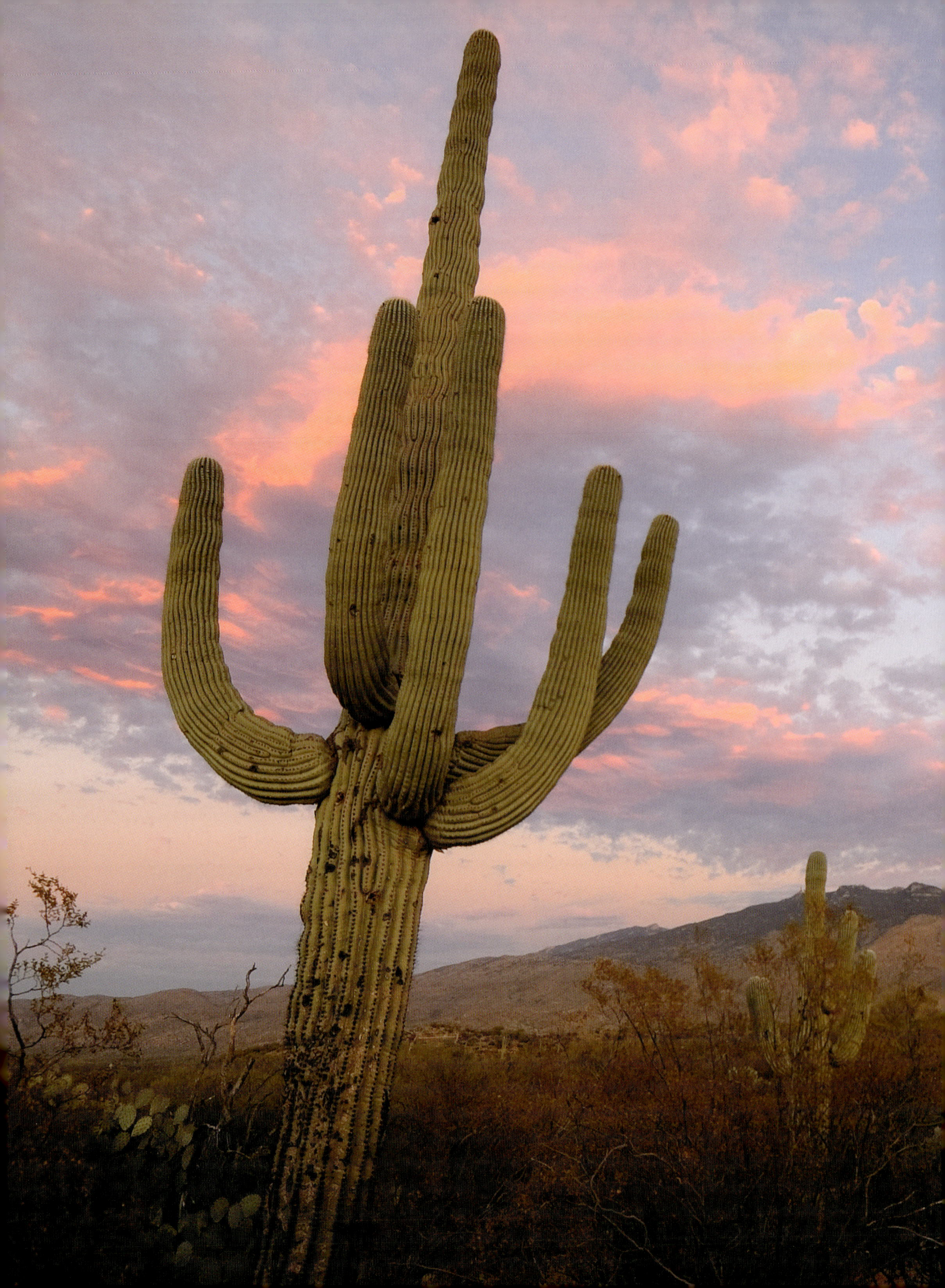

In Father Kino's Footsteps
✯ ✯ ✯ Nogales to Tucson, Arizona ✯ ✯ ✯ ✯ ✯ ✯ ✯

In 1691, Pimería Alta's ragged frontier marked the practical limits of New Spain in the vast territory between Santa Fe and the California coast. Tucson was the last outpost in a chain stretching back to Mexico City. Without obvious riches for colonists to extract, the enormous task of introducing Spanish and Catholic authority to the Sonoran region was relegated to Jesuit missionaries.

Generations of Pima (Akimel O'odham) and Papago (Tohono O'odham) Indians traveled the Santa Cruz River corridor long before Father Eusebio Kino first ventured northward. Kino, an astronomer, cartographer and mathematician, had hoped the Jesuit order would send him to China. Instead, the Italian-born priest was dispatched to Sonora, from where he made more than 40 expeditions, disproving along the way the belief that Baja California was an island. He learned cattle ranching at his first missionary assignment in old Mexico, and drove in Arizona's first herds from the missions of upper Sonora.

Kino's earliest journey into modern-day Arizona reached only to Tumacácori, where he proselytized in 1691. The Santa Cruz River to its confluence with the Gila River became a highway for Kino as he extended his mission network and probed westward for an overland route to California. Vulnerable to hostile attacks, particularly from mounted Apaches, missionary outposts were consolidated at places like Tumacácori, Geuvavi and the isolated San Xavier del Bac. By the end of his life in 1711, Kino had survived three desert crossings via the "route of the Devil," discovered the Hohokam ruins at Casa Grande, and defined a route that became the first 60 miles of Highway 89.

The Tumacácori mission itself is the best preserved of three ruins at the Tumacácori National Historic Park and the only one accessible to the public. This National Park Service unit is one of the quietest in Arizona, with an annual visitation comparable to a summer weekend at Grand Canyon National Park. Once a year, area residents fill the

SAGUARO NATIONAL PARK: Sunset at the eastern unit of Saguaro National Park in Tucson illuminates a wildlife oasis wrapped on three sides by urban development. (opposite)

SPINY HORNED TOAD: Local flora and fauna are carved into the entryway stonework of St. Augustine Cathedral in Tucson. (above)

US HIGHWAY 89: ARIZONA ✯ 15

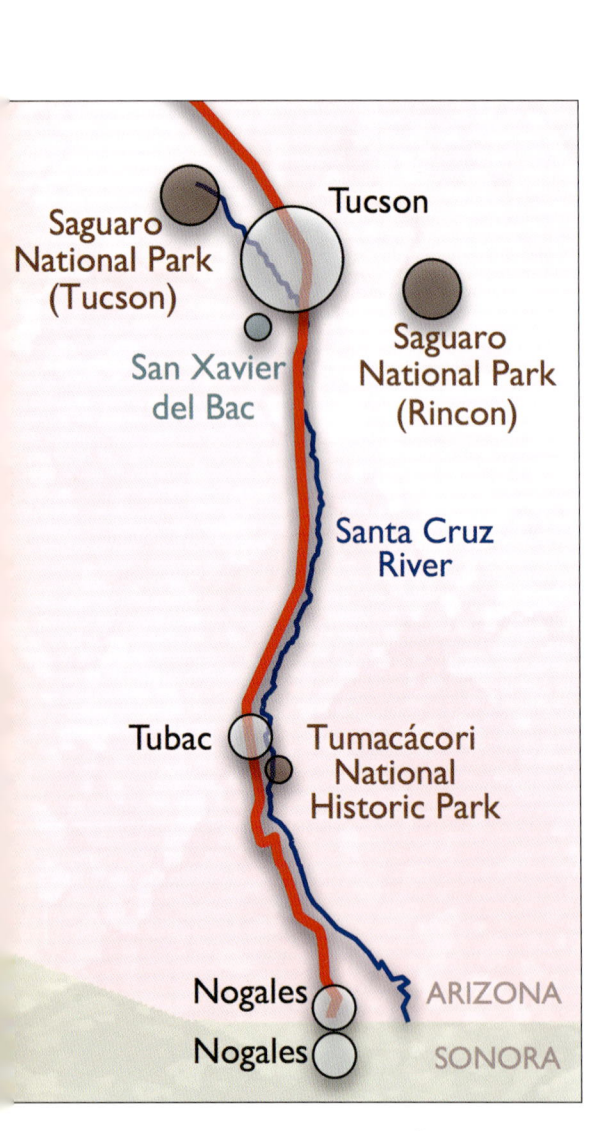

plaza to celebrate a mariachi mass for the feast of St. Francis Xavier. The service begins with an elaborate procession of Yaqui and Tohono O'odham tribal members, who greet uniformed park rangers and re-enactors wearing colonial-era costumes.

Local participants also sustain a uniquely Southwestern Christmas Eve tradition at Tumacácori. At sunset, volunteers light thousands of paper lanterns set on the walls and recesses of the church, while a park ranger wearing a Santa cap plays carols on his guitar for the waiting crowd. The gates open as the sky dims to a lapis blue as the luminaria guide visitors into the candle-lit church.

San Xavier del Bac Mission

Kino established a mission at San Xavier del Bac, but built no church there. In 1767, papal and European secular power struggles spilled into the colonies, as King Charles of Spain expelled the independent Jesuits from his dominion. The Franciscan order, under secular control of the crown, took over the Sonoran frontier missions. These monks and Tohono O'odham craftsmen completed the church now known as the "White Dove of the Desert" in 1797, almost 100 years after Kino's first visit.

St. Francis Xavier, Kino's patron saint, was also an energetic missionary. He evangelized from his native Spain to India, Indonesia and Japan. After his 1552 death en route to China, Francis Xavier was canonized along with Ignatius of Loyola as the first Jesuit saints. The recumbent pose of his statue in San Xavier del Bac recalls the miraculous preservation of his body when it was returned to India 150 years after his death. A similar, full-sized figure of the saint also reposes in the Magdalena, Sonora, church where Kino himself is buried.

Today, San Xavier del Bac's towering adobe walls and lavish interiors draw thousands of visitors. The church and parochial school continue to serve an active congregation on the Tohono O'odham reservation. Parishioners celebrate the feast of St. Francis Xavier in their own December festival. And each October 4th, thousands make

FIESTA CROSS: Tumacácori National Historic Park hosts only one public mass a year. The Tumacácori Fiesta is closed to photography at the request of the tribal community participants. Elements of the mass are celebrated in English, Spanish, Yaqui and Tohono O'odham. During the 2006 processional of park service employees, priests, and native dancers, this cross (opposite) was carried to the doors of the church at the start of the service.

CHRISTMAS EVE: Tumacácori National Historic Park volunteers place candle-lit luminaria on the walls of the ruins to celebrate Christmas Eve. (above)

US Highway 89: Arizona ★ 17

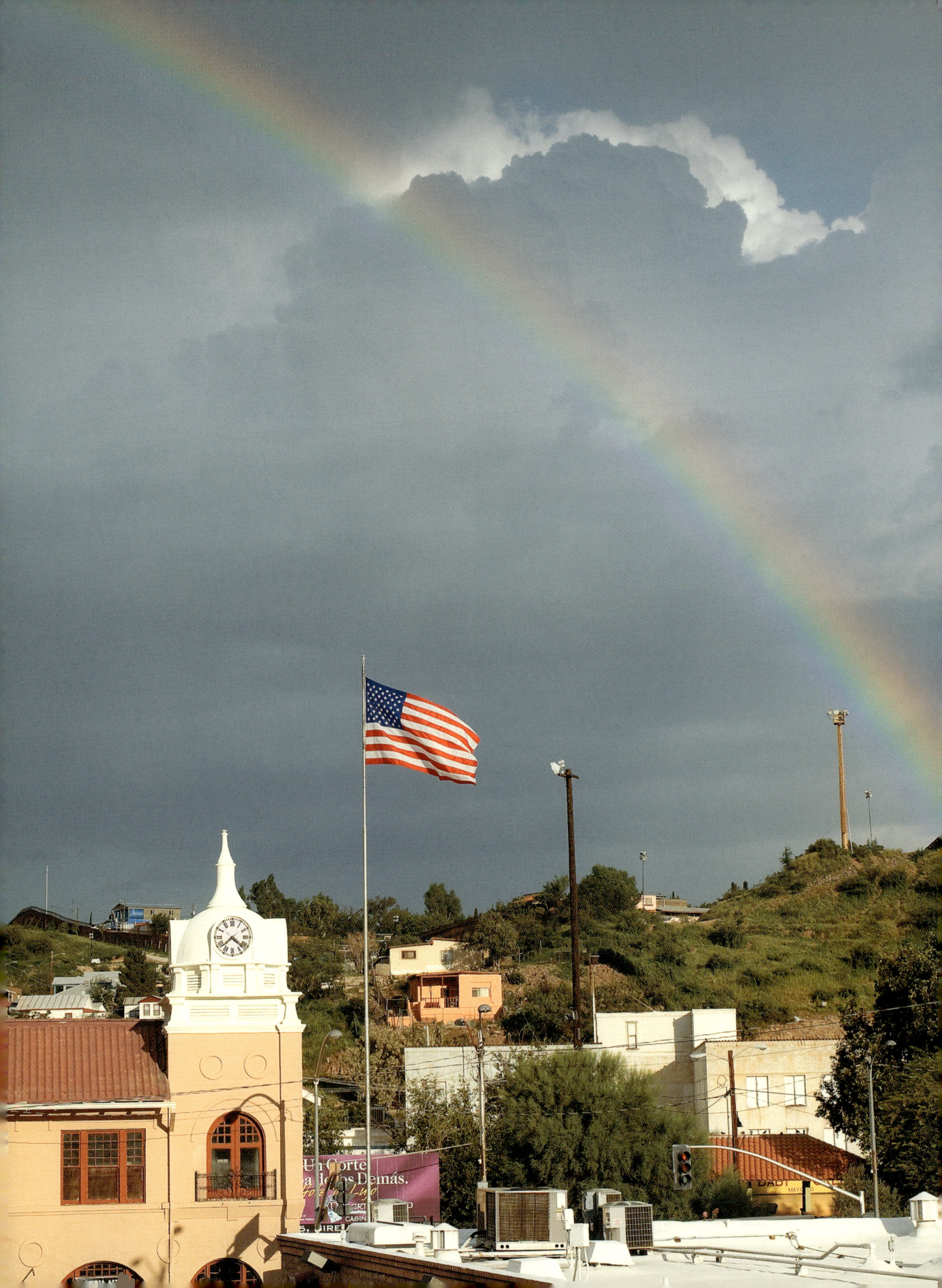
Demás.

pilgrimages to Magdalena (the Franciscan priests shifted the feast day, perhaps to steer veneration to that of their own St. Francis of Assisi). Some of the faithful cross the border to begin their trek at Nogales, a few walk over one hundred miles from San Xavier del Bac.

Tucson

In the 1848 treaty that ended the Mexican-American war, Mexico retained the territory south of the Gila River, including Tucson. As American army engineers began surveying the region for an all-season transcontinental railway route, their maps indicated that the best route passed well south of the river. James Gadsden, ambassador to Mexico (and president of a South Carolina regional railway), negotiated the 1853 Gadsden Purchase that defined today's southern boundary of the lower 48 states.

The intervening Civil War and post-war economic collapse delayed construction of the Southern Pacific Railway into Arizona, but when the tracks arrived, Tucson became the region's largest city. The railway located a major repair facility there, while the mainline bypassed Phoenix entirely. A huge ice-making plant sat next to Tucson's rails to supply refrigerator cars laden with citrus and vegetables from California and Mexico.

The Southern Pacific even delivered Arizona's first automobile. Dr. Hiram Fenner paid $600 (plus $200 shipping) for his Locomobile in 1899. Many of Fenner's patients came to Tucson in search of a dry climate cure for tuberculous, a disease afflicting some 10 percent of the American population. Wealthy patients sought treatment in sanatoriums, the poor suffered in tent camps. St. Mary's Hospital, operated by the Sisters of St. Joseph of Carondelet, commissioned Fenner to build a facility to serve the many "lungers" who needed care.

AMBOS NOGALES: A rainbow arcs over the Old Nogales City Hall. The U.S.–Mexican border fence runs along the hillside within a few yards of private residences on either side of the divide. (opposite)

SOLO MARCH: John Dillon (left) walked the length of the U.S.–Mexico border region while pulling a cross on skateboard wheels to advocate both for border security and a compassionate approach toward undocumented immigrants.

ROADSIDE ATTRACTION: Wisdom Cafe's trademark chicken (above) fronts the old Nogales Highway segment of U.S. 89.

SHADOWING THE FUTURE: Scaffolding around the west tower casts shadows on the dome during the church renovation (above); CHAPEL ENTRY (below); INTERIOR VIEW (opposite), all San Xavier del Bac Mission.

To promote the town as a destination for healthy vacationers and new residents, local Dodge dealer Jesse James launched the Tucson Sunshine Climate Club in 1922. Funded by voluntary contributions, the group advertised nationally and hired a full-time staff to answer inquiries and greet newcomers. In 1923, 17 winter guests arrived on a single October day.

Ambos Nogales

Ambos Nogales refers to the twin cities at the U.S.–Mexico border, named for an encampment used by the international boundary commission in 1855 while demarcating the Gadsden Purchase border. In the 1880s, the Atchison, Topeka & Santa Fe Railway began building tracks from the Mexican port of Guaymas to Nogales, and ultimately the American transcontinental system. A minor settlement rush launched the border town, despite the fact that legacy Mexican land grants encumbered city incorporation for another decade. The first railway shipments from Mexico brought oranges to Tucson in 1910, the same year hostilities erupted in the Mexican revolution.

Rebel Mexican armies controlled much of northern Sonora, fighting near and across the border. Pancho Villa's band played a

20 ★ IN FATHER KINO'S FOOTSTEPS

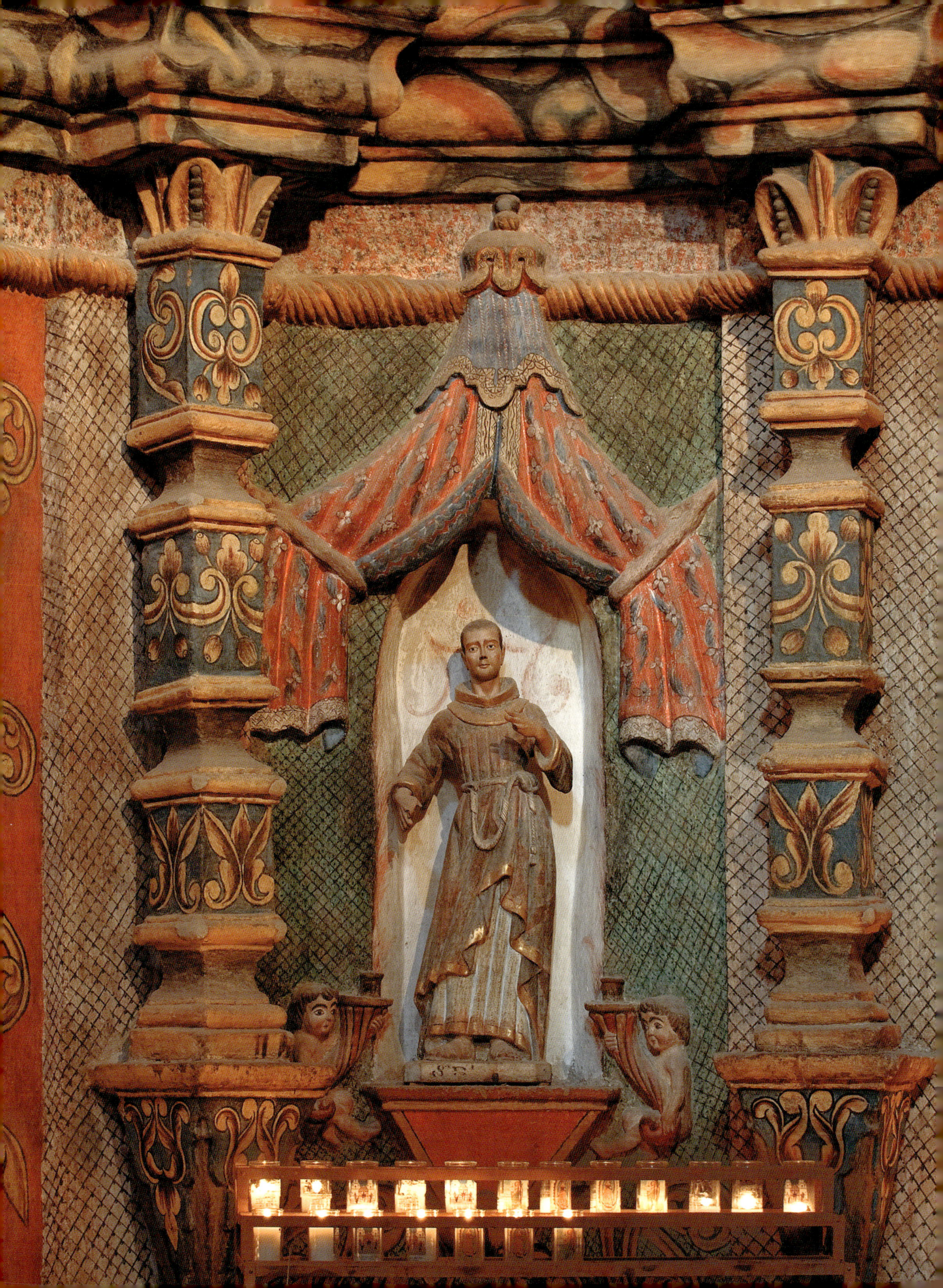

concert in a Nogales, Arizona, park in 1914. Two years later General John D. Pershing was pursuing Villa throughout Sonora. Leery of cross-border skirmishes, the Sonoran governor, not the Americans, ordered installation of an 11-strand wire fence in 1917. International tensions eased when President Woodrow Wilson recalled the American troops and Pershing took command of the Allied Forces in World War I.

The revolutionary conflict so destabilized the Mexican political and economic structure that, from 1910 to 1930, one in ten Mexican adults emigrated to the U.S. At the same time, post-war American attitudes toward immigration soured. Quotas were enacted in 1920, supported by unions fearful of labor competition, and by conservatives who worried about cultural changes that might result from large numbers of Catholic Polish and Italian immigrants. In Arizona, the 1924 creation of the Border Patrol met with immediate conflict from cotton growers accustomed to hiring migrant Mexican field workers.

Commerce, customs and border control continue to dominate the Ambos Nogales communities. Mexican nationals contribute about 60 percent of sales taxes collected in Nogales, Arizona. At Christmas time, the streets of both towns are filled with international shoppers who cross through a pedestrian check point. All winter, columns of semi-trucks convey fresh fruits and vegetables northward: 60 percent of the produce consumed by Americans and Canadians passes through Nogales. The flows of wind and river, of course, respect no political boundary, and joint cooperation has begun to attack environmental problems like the water effluent quality in the Santa Cruz River and diesel-generated smog from vehicles idling at the border crossing.

Saguaro National Park
Of the seven national parks along historic Highway 89, Saguaro is the youngest, one of the smallest (Bryce National Park is smaller) and the only one bordered by a major metropolitan area. Decades of cactus rustling and cattle grazing decimating the saguaro population provided the impetus for creation of Saguaro National Monument. The 1933 declaration included only 63,300 acres in the foothills of the Rincon Mountains; a second unit 30 miles to the west was added in 1961. As Tucson's development reached the park boundaries, the U.S. Congress elevated the unit to national park status in 1994.

A rarity of killing frosts separates the Sonoran ecosystem from other North American deserts. Plant and animal communities are specially adapted for prolonged hot summers and dual winter and monsoon rainy seasons, which wet the area with only about 12 inches of moisture in two equal installments.

Sentinels of the Sonoran desert, saguaros advanced

northward into Arizona only 8,000 years ago, following the retreat of the last ice age. From root stock only 3 inches deep and spreading as wide as its longest branches, a saguaro can eventually grow to 50 feet and weigh eight tons. Its roots can absorb an entire year's water needs from one penetrating rain. But the saguaro is a slow grower: it may take 30 years to flower and 75 years to develop its first branch.

Many of the park's animal species rely on the saguaro. Bats nectar on its night-opening flowers. Gila woodpeckers drill nesting hollows in the trunks each year and elf owls reuse the old cavities, while cactus wrens build nests in the crooks of branches. Native bees cross-pollinate the flowers, which remain open into the next morning.

The Tohono O'odham people used the saguaros' woody ribs to construct shelters and harvested their nutritious seeds, which contain up to 30 percent fat. The fruit's juicy red pulp ripens at the end of June, during the hottest, driest, hungriest time of the year. The Tohono O'odham began their calendar at the saguaro fruit harvest, fermenting the juices for a ceremony to bring summer monsoons to water their fields and sustain them for another year.

Mariachi
Musicians in miniature charro suits stream backstage before the student showcase at the Tucson International Mariachi Conference. Parents follow, staggering under stacks of black sombreros. The hats are distributed to 50 elementary students from Davis Bilingual Magnet School while their maestro silences the giggling troop and gives last-minute instructions.

The youngsters are all business when they take the stage. For three days, some of the world's foremost musicians have instructed them on their instruments, showmanship and mariachi traditions. Professional mariachi bands, the students learned, have a repertoire of at least 1,000 songs. Tonight's audience includes many grandparents who sing along to all the numbers. Kids trade solos with choruses from the band. A little red-headed violinist sings her verse of "God Bless America" in Spanish. Another pre-teen guittarrón player with a huge stage presence struts with the microphone during his solo and wins over the crowd.

Like the traje suit (short jacket, tight trousers with rows of silver buttons, boots and hat), the mariachi tradition originates from Jalisco, in the heart of Mexico's ranching country. Over time, some of the more masculine aspects have been adapted for a new generation of performers. Female players substitute a long skirt decorated with botonadura for the gentlemen's trousers. Some of the high school groups embroider each student's name on his or her enormous bow tie.

Student groups have been playing mariachi in Tucson since the late 1960s, when Father Charles Rourke, himself a jazz pianist, started the Changeitos Feos (Ugly Monkeys) ensemble as an after-school program. In 1983, mariachi fans teamed with local non-profit health center La Frontera to stage the first conference. Today, an international cast of stars performs at a benefit concert with the conference students. Ticket sales have raised $3.5 million for La Frontera's children's services, and the maestros conduct workshops for more than 1,000 student participants each year. Twenty-five years later, conference graduates return as instructors and Arizona's universities offer student scholarships to their mariachi programs.

Motoring on U.S. 89
Since the 1920s, Tucsonans have promoted everything from polo, rodeo, western movie-making and a museum in a Titan Missile silo to encourage motorists to stop in their town. In 1938, a real estate promoter came up with "Miracle Mile" to describe an improved stretch of Highway 89 on the northern outskirts of town. This most modern intersection in Arizona warranted a feature in *Arizona Highways*, which noted its 22 foot wide lanes, 38 foot median and landscaping. Family-run tourist camps and travel courts clustered at the crossroads to receive the motoring public.

When Interstate 10 bypassed the Highway 89 route to Phoenix, and as travelers opted for motel chains along the interstate, the Miracle Mile area declined. Many of the relic travel courts are simply boarded up. A few function as low income housing and weekly motels. One establishment has been renamed: old Highway 89 can claim an actual "No-tel Motel."

A far more reputable family-run establishment, El Charro Cafe, has served Tucsonans for 85 years. Located in the walled Presidio district, the restaurant is filled with founder Monica Flin's treasures, from her father's rifles to poster-sized calendars distributed by the restaurant since the 1930s. El Charro tells Tucson's story through the Flin family, and the menu notes an uncle's objection to including the nacho plate, mere ballpark food, on a list of authentic Tucson dishes.

From the historic barrio neighborhood, Highway 89 heads north beyond the old Spanish frontier. A narrowing contour of strip-malls and subdivisions lies beneath the Santa Catalina Mountains. At the limit of civilization, just as in Kino's time, the expanse of the desert awaits. Cacti and the occasional cow border the road to Florence, as Highway 89 leaves behind a uniquely Tucson blend of Hispanic and western American heritage.

FIESTA DE GARIBALDI: Elementary school bands share the stage with mariachi groups from across the Southwest at the final day of the Tucson International Mariachi Conference. (opposite)

CENTRAL BARRIO DISTRICT: The historic district of Tucson retains its Spanish heritage with a multicultural twist. This adobe home (left) is located just outside the walls of the Spanish presidio, blocks away from the cathedral, city hall and one of Tucson's oldest Mexican restaurants. A representation of the Hindu elephant god Ganesha decorates the entry.

FOX THEATRE: Experts replicated the original 1930 marquee sign (above) during the 1999–2006 renovation of Tucson's landmark downtown theatre, now a venue for films and live performances.

VIEW FROM THE TOP: Sunrise from the Santa Catalina Mountains above Tucson (preceding pages)

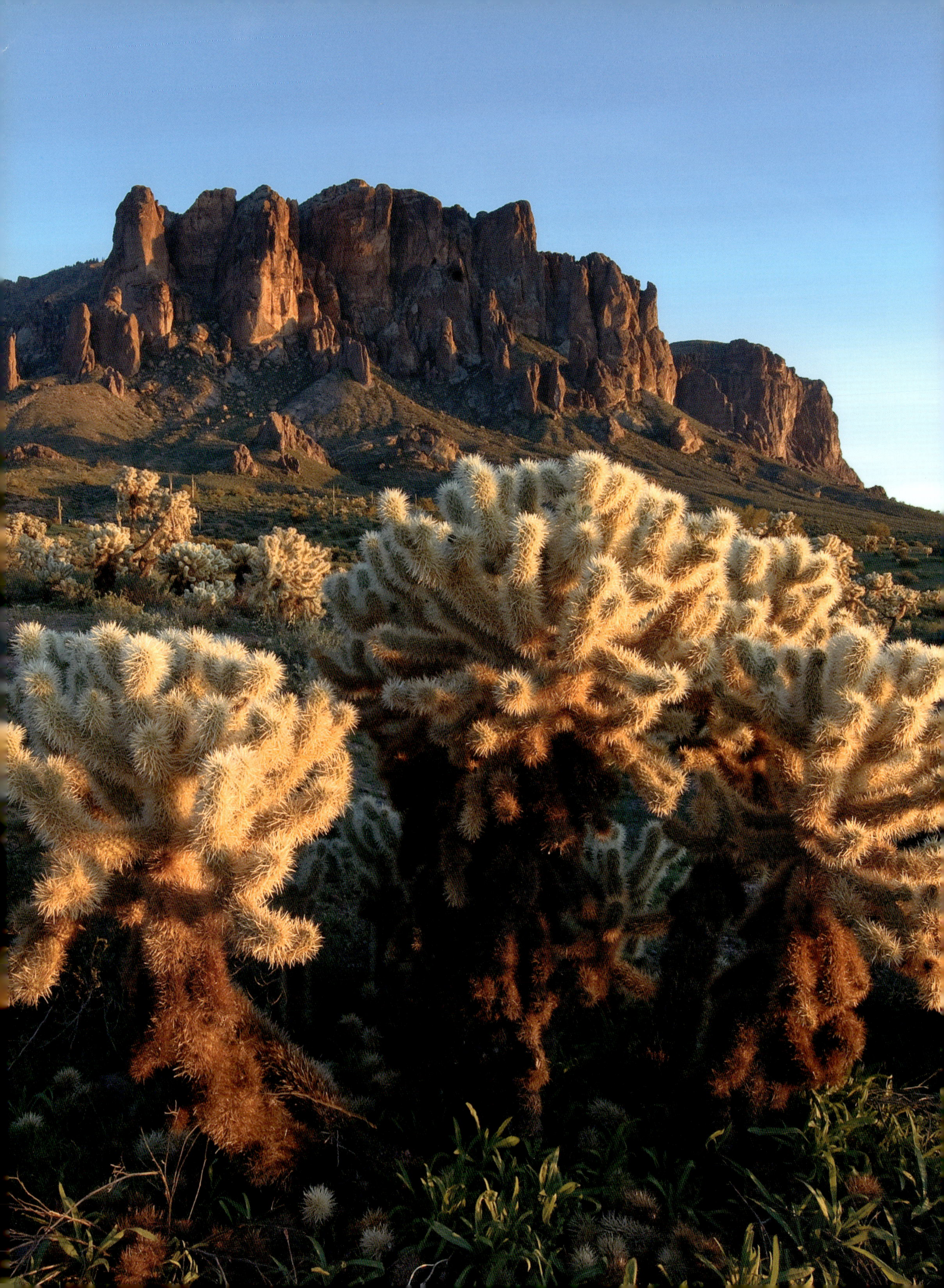

Arizona's First Highway
★ ★ ★ Tucson to Route 66, Arizona ★ ★ ★ ★ ★ ★ ★ ★ ★

Arizona's first highway curved across its deserts like a lizard's backbone. By 1925, most of the future U.S. 89 from Tucson to Flagstaff had been surfaced, if not paved. The state highway engineer announced in the first issue of *Arizona Highways* that construction on Yarnell Hill would shorten the distance from Phoenix to Prescott by 26.54 miles.

Tucson's Spanish pioneers oriented their cultural compass to the south. Arizona's first Anglos trickled in, then streamed, from all directions. In the wake of fur trappers came California forty-niners and battalions on both sides of the Civil War. Prospectors began to explore Arizona's mineral wealth. Huge gold strikes, like the 1863 discovery at Weaver Creek, where the ground surface yielded $100,000 in three months, drew miners into the heart of Yavapai Indian country. The inevitable hostilities and settlers' demands for protection soon led the U.S. Army to establish Fort Whipple, seeding the growth of Prescott, Arizona's territorial capitol.

Both Anglos and Mexicans settled on the rivers between Tucson and Prescott, supplying miners with farm crops, whiskey and other essential needs. The difficulty of transporting goods across the desert limited Arizona's early growth as much as the lack of water. The U.S. Army tried camels instead of mules; the animals proved suitable for carrying heavy loads, but the wrangler-soldiers resisted innovation. Only highly valuable cargos, like gold and silver, were shipped any distance by mule wagons. Without efficient transportation, Arizona's extractive resources, like timber and copper, remained largely untapped.

SUPERSTITION MOUNTAINS: Lost Dutchman State Park (opposite)

OPUNTIA BLOSSOM (above)

Poston's Butte (Florence, Arizona)

"From the town are visible Poston Butte in the northwest directly across the Gila River; the palisades of Superstition Mountain on the northern horizon; and chains of grotesque points and buttes in the

east. Backed by cloud banks these peaks resemble nineteenth century Biblical drawings illustrating a rendezvous of displeased deity with mortal man." (from Arizona: The Grand Canyon State*)**

The last of the lower 48 states to be admitted to the Union, Arizona had many champions, but few as colorful as Charles D. Poston. Poston was a shipwreck survivor, silver mine promoter, even alcalde of Tubac (performing marriages and baptisms). As a Washington, D.C., aide in President Abraham Lincoln's administration, Poston lobbied for the creation of the Arizona Territory, and was elected

---

* Well-known Depression-era relief programs built federal highways, bridges and national park facilities. Another Works Progress Administration effort, the Federal Writers Project, hired white collar and clerical workers to produce guidebooks for every state and the Alaskan territory. The "American Guide Series" described each state's natural history, cultural and economic background, folklore and the arts, and outlined mile-by-mile auto tours of the new federal highway system. First appearing in 1937, the books were often revised by the states; a few are still in print.

its first delegate to the U.S. Congress. After his term, he traveled through Europe and India, where he was initiated into the rites of sun worship. Returning to Arizona in 1877, he built a pyre outside of Florence on a butte that he named Parsee Hill. He kept the fire burning for several months; onlookers called it Poston's Folly. He moved to Tucson and then Nogales, drifting into obscurity and poverty, though the territorial government voted him a pension in 1899. Poston died in Phoenix three years later. In a 1925 ceremony led by Arizona's governor, Poston was reinterred on Parsee Hill. On the butte now named for the "Father of Arizona," a large stone pyramid marks Poston's grave.

Basin and Range

Highway 89's route from Tucson to Yarnell skirts between numerous mountain ranges. Vantage points like Poston's Butte reveal the underlying structure of Arizona's Basin and Range topography. Only eight million years ago, the Pacific fault plate moved away from the North American continent, stretching and fracturing the earth's mantle from Idaho to Mexico into bands of parallel blocks. Alternating segments sank as much as 10,000 feet into the molten crust; subsequent erosion from adjacent blocks filled the valleys

BIOSPHERE 2: From 1991 to 1993, eight scientists lived sealed within the Biosphere 2 research station (opposite) north of Tucson, studying agriculture and human impacts within closed ecosystems, like future space stations. Now leased to the University of Arizona for large-scale experiments on climate change, the facility is open for public tours.

FLORENCE PRISON RUN: For over 25 years, the Hells Angels Motorcycle Clubs of Arizona have organized the Florence Prison Run (above). Originating as a show of support for an incarcerated member, today over 1,000 motorcyclists from across the region meet each year in Florence to ride past the state prison.

30 ★ Arizona's First Highway

with sediments 5,000 feet thick. The highest mountain ranges, like the Catalina Mountains north of Tucson, support temperate plant and animal communities, but the highway itself traverses a landscape dominated by Sonoran Desert biota.

On the Yarnell Hill grade (the last section of Highway 89 to Ashfork to be completed), the road climbs 2,500 feet in six miles. From Yarnell Hill, the route enters Arizona's Central Highlands, a geologic transition area rich in minerals and blanketed with upland grasslands, piñon woodlands and ponderosa pine forests that extend to the Colorado Plateau.

The Five "Cs" of Arizona
Gold and silver made a few pioneers' fortunes, but real economic growth blossomed with major investments for infrastructure and transportation. Generations of Arizona school children learned the five Cs that drove their state's economy: copper, cattle, cotton, citrus and climate. Mining Arizona's copper became profitable once railway branches linked them to processing sites and markets. Even as the Atlantic & Pacific Railway (later the Atchison, Topeka & Santa Fe Railway) and the Southern Pacific Railway raced to build their transcontinental lines to California's ports, both looked to mining areas to assure steady freight revenues.

Cheap railway freight also opened the territory to large-scale cattle-grazing. Ranchers found they could turn unlimited numbers of cattle onto virgin public grazing lands. By the early 1890s, 1.5 million head were on the range, and overgrazing had permanently altered

GOLD RUSH COUNTRY: (opposite, clockwise from top left) Gunslinger gear at Wickenburg Gold Rush Days; Wickenburg's Garter Girls; Frog Rock, near Congress; in the 1860s and 1870s, Wickenburg residents chained their convicts to the Jail Tree, this now 200-year-old mesquite tree; the U.S. Post Office offered commemorative stamp cancellations for Wickenburg's 60th annual Gold Rush Days.

LAST SUPPER: Yarnell Native American artist Felix Lucero sculpted the life-sized *Jesus Christ at the Last Supper* (above) as part of the Shrine of St. Joseph, commissioned in 1939 by a group of Catholic lay people from Phoenix. The pilgrimage site also features the Stations of the Cross, with Lucero's carving of Christ's tomb hollowed into the hillside.

PHOENIX SKYLINE: The Security Building, at the corner of Central and Van Buren (formerly Highway 89), was Phoenix's (and Arizona's) tallest building when its first eight stories were completed in 1929. The penthouse was added in 1958. Today, the top floors house the Phoenix Urban Research Laboratory, part of Arizona State University's expansion campus, which is helping to revitalize downtown Phoenix. (right)

DESERT-STYLE HOLIDAY: Glendale (above)

WATERWORKS: When Phoenix construction crews on the Arizona Canal ran into bedrock in 1884, the builders did not want to delay the construction to blast it out and Arizona Falls was born. The 2003 WaterWorks project (opposite) blended public open space with a modernization of the hydroelectric plant, first installed in 1902. One early feature restored in the project was a neighborhood dance floor above the falls.

TEMPE TOWN LAKE: Architecture students at Arizona State University in 1966 first conceived of an artificial lake at the center of Tempe's urban master plan. Over several stages and 33 years, the town created green belts, bike paths and a walkable commercial zone as part of the Rio Salado Project. Each year, traffic is diverted from the Mill Avenue bridges on New Year's Eve to launch the fireworks that cap off the pre-Fiesta Bowl celebrations. (page 34)

soil stability and drainage patterns in the fragile desert ecosystem. Droughts and increased railway freight prices brought the Arizona cattle industry to near collapse. Ranching resumed at a smaller scale, reorganized as the federal government began to exert control through grazing permits, despite the resistance from old-timers who believed "public lands" meant unregulated use.

Crops and Canals

Cotton and citrus, Arizona's hallmark crops, depended not only on efficient transportation to eastern markets, but on the ability to deliver water through yet another C: canals.

The Hohokam people, the region's first agriculturalists, depended entirely on irrigated agriculture. Using only stone tools and human labor, they dug canals as long as 20 miles and as deep as 20 feet. The earliest waterworks go back as far as AD 50; by AD 600, the Hohokam were engineering massive projects. One canal at the Pueblo Grande ruins in Phoenix irrigated as much as 10,000 acres. At its peak, the Hohokam established communities along the Gila, Salt and Verde rivers and spread to the Santa Cruz River basin near Tucson. The civilization collapsed before the arrival of Columbus, which archeologists suggest was due to a combination of ecological factors and resource depletion. Untended for centuries, the Hohokam canal banks gradually eroded and refilled its channels.

Four hundred years later, Confederate soldier Jack Swilling arrived in the Arizona Territory just as the Union Army marched in from California. The rebels retreated to Texas; Swilling remained. As a civilian he carried dispatches for the Union Army and guided prospecting expeditions. With Paulino Weaver and A.H. Peebles, Swilling led the party that discovered gold at Rich Hill in 1863, providing him with a substantial fortune. Fascinated by the Hohokam ruins in the Salt River Valley, he conceived of a plan to re-excavate the ancient canals and grow crops for mining and army camps. In December 1867, Swilling organized an investment company to finance his scheme, and within four months, water was flowing and the first crops were harvested.

As people settled the Phoenix area, the original name for Swilling's settlement, Pumpkintown, did not survive. More canals followed: in 1878, Mormon pioneers renovated some of the Hohokam works near Mesa. Today, nine main canals and more than 900 miles of "laterals" deliver agricultural water across the Phoenix valley. Irrigating the desert generated an agricultural boom and soon refrigerated railway cars were shipping luxury crops, like strawberries, figs and dates, in addition to cotton and citrus fruits.

Lakes in the Desert

"About eighteen miles northeast of Wickenburg on the Hassayampa River was Walnut Grove Dam,

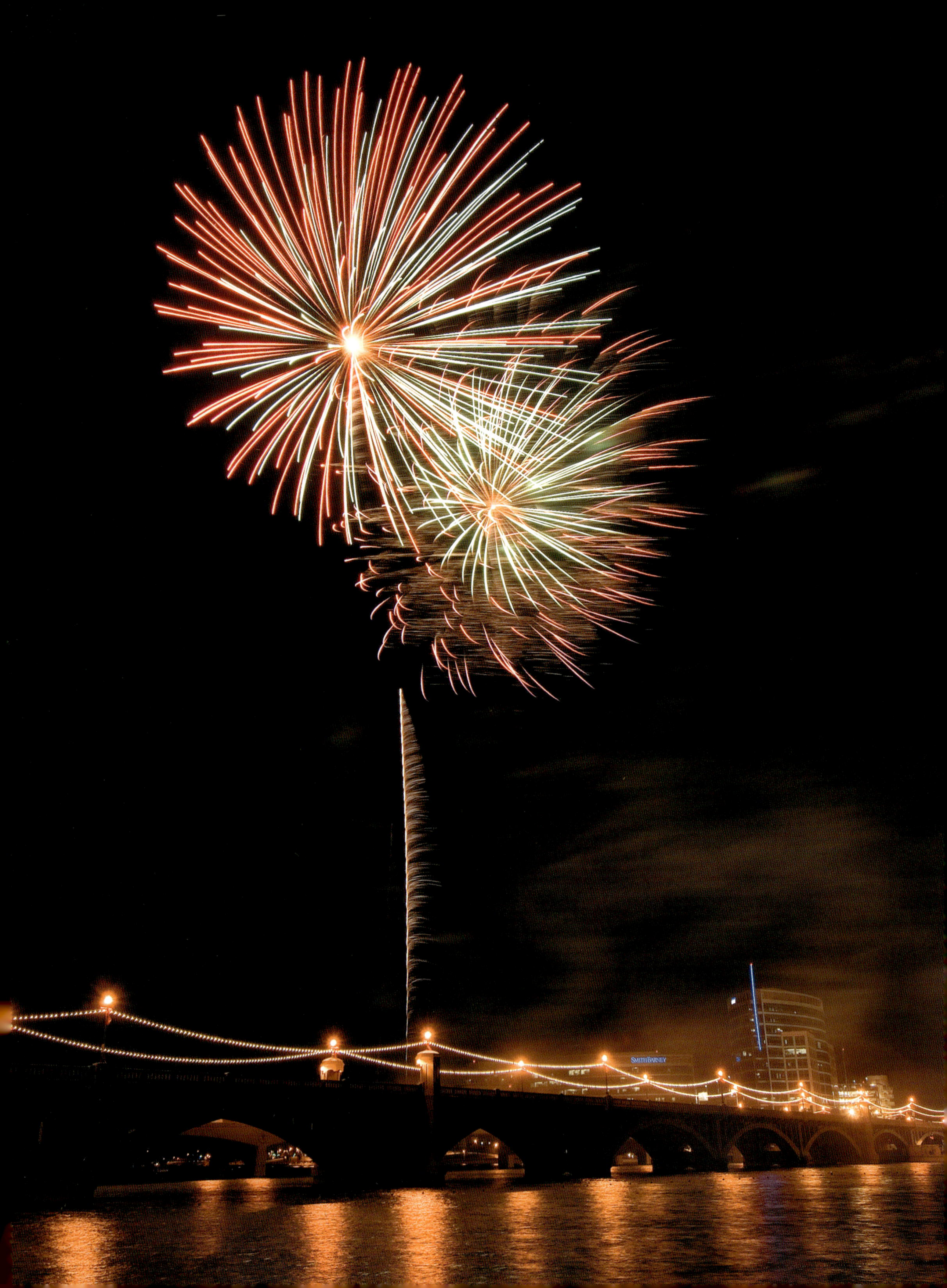

long since washed away. Known to be of weak construction, the dam was being strengthened and an additional spillway to carry off flood water was being built in 1890, when a terrific rainstorm caused fear for the safety of the people in the lower valley. A rider mounted a swift horse and set out to warn those in danger, but stopped at the first saloon for a drink and lingered. The flood broke the dam and washed away the saloon with those inside. A heavy steel safe containing five thousand dollars in gold dust was never found, nor was the rider who had delayed." (Arizona: The Grand Canyon State*)*

Arizona's new farmers, like the ancient Hohokam, had to cope with alternating droughts and floods. Controlling the flow of water was essential not only for prosperity, but to ensure Arizonans' safety: flooding has caused some of the state's worst natural disasters. The 1890 Walnut Grove Dam failure resulted in 128 deaths. That same February day in Phoenix, the Salt River rose 17 feet in 15 hours. A year later, the river crested again in a flood almost three miles wide, demolishing homes and the railway bridge that linked Phoenix to the Southern Pacific mainline.

Damming Arizona's major rivers required federal financing and construction, which was authorized in the National Reclamation Act of 1902. President Theodore Roosevelt inaugurated the first major dam on the Salt River in 1911. His party motored along the Apache Trail (and future Highway 89) to Roosevelt Lake, once the world's largest man-made lake.

Watersports in the desert seem incongruous, but Arizona has one of the highest concentration of motorboats per resident of any state. The state's many artificial lakes provide recreational outlets for its rapidly growing population. While most of the lakes are outside urban centers, Tempe Town Lake was designed to bring the waterfront to the people and to transform the cityscape in the process. A 1966 architecture class at Arizona State University first proposed to dam the Salt River as the centerpiece for Tempe's downtown redevelopment. Acquiring water rights, engineering a new style of dam with rubber components and funding the construction took decades: not until 1999 did water top the spillways. At the same time, Tempe redesigned the adjacent Mill Avenue area to encourage a walkable downtown. This stretch of old Highway 89 now boasts outdoor cafes; new office buildings and condominiums line the waterfront; and a marina encourages fishing, sculling and sailing. Each New Year's Eve, fireworks launched from the old Mill Avenue bridge wow the 100,000 spectators at the Fiesta Bowl's pre-game party.

Flocks of Snowbirds
"In winter, thousands of visitors from other states and Europe crowd the streets and speed up the town. Highlighting the tourist season is the Salad Bowl Parade and Football Game, the morning parade of beautiful floats, beauty queens, high school and college bands from over the state vie for prizes, and the New Year's Day game is between teams of national prominence." (from Arizona: The Grand Canyon State*)*

Although freight accounted for the bulk of their revenues, transcontinetal railways heavily promoted Arizona as a vacation destination. Tucson, Phoenix and other towns nationally advertised their sunny, dry winters. Arizonans capitalized on its fifth "C," climate, by offering a new style of recreation targeted to tourists eager to experience the romance of the west. Enterprising ranching families established dude ranches, turning "greenhorns" into fantasy camp cowhands. Arizona's first guest ranch opened in 1913 at the Garden of Allah and nearby Wickenburg became a dude ranching mecca. Some of the early guest ranches remain, although the date palms that tower among the cottonwoods at the Garden of Allah site are now part of The Nature Conservancy's Hassayampa River Preserve.

Visiting dudes, city slickers and ranching families mingled together at rodeos in Tucson, Phoenix and Wickenburg during the peak winter social season. Everyone could (and should) "Go Western" in cowboy hats and boots for the parade, parties and arena events. Prescott organized the world's first public rodeo in 1888, taming the cowboys' street-side contests of skill (and gambling and brawling aftermath) into a Fourth of July tradition.

BATHING BEAUTIES: In the 1950s, a string of motels lined the Apache Trail east of Phoenix. Colorful neon advertised amenities, such as swimming pools. The divers in this sign light up in a three beat succession, culminating in a splash.

Across the Sun Belt, cities promoted special events to attract tourists to the mild winter climate. To compete with Pasadena's Rose Bowl and Miami's Orange Bowl, Phoenix launched its own college bowl game in 1948. The Salad Bowl series ran only five years. Nineteen years later, hometown favorite Arizona State University won the inaugural Fiesta Bowl match.

A Phoenix civic group, the Dons Club, organized a more whimsical annual tradition: a search for the Lost Dutchman gold mine. If the mine ever existed, it was lost by the Mexican Peralta family, not by Jacob Waltz, a German, not Dutch, immigrant at the center of the legend. On his 1891 deathbed, Waltz declared that a wagon carrying gold from Peralta's workings had been attacked by Apaches, the mine abandoned, and that the sole survivor had told Waltz the mine's location. Waltz's caregivers found a cache of gold under his bed; some say he drew a map for them before he died. Folklorists have long speculated that Waltz's gold actually came from mines near Wickenburg rather than the Superstition Mountains. Dozens claimed to have rediscovered the mine, a few even displayed some gold, but the Dons had the most fun with the story. Tourists made reservations weeks in advance for the trek. Sporting Spanish gentry-inspired costumes, the Dons and their wives, their donkeys (packing water barrels and provisions) and guests never found the mine, perhaps distracted each year by the Mexican dancers, cowboy musicians and campfire at trail's end.

The Yavapai

"The Yavapai, part of the Yuman family, have declined until there are only seventy members. They have neither traditions nor a culture of their own. All records of their early existence have been lost and they are glad to forget the past, which as they explain, consisted only of hardship." (from Arizona: The Grand Canyon State*)*

The traditional Yavapai territory encompassed nearly 10 million acres of Arizona's harshest desert. The challenging terrain deterred Spanish conquest, and the Yavapai had not adopted European weaponry prior to their 1863 contact with Anglos. Traveling long distances in their annual harvest of wild foods, hunting and crops, their migratory cycle was quickly disrupted by the settlers, who demanded the tribe's removal to reservations, if not outright extermination.

After a 10-year army campaign, General George Crook restricted the remaining Yavapai to the Rio Verde Reservation. Hardships for the tribe persisted. One-third of them died on the reservation; the survivors scraped out a five-mile long irrigation ditch using worn and rusty Army tools. Their bountiful harvest only caused more misery: government contractors, denied profits on ration sales, campaigned to have the Yavapai moved to the Apache reservation at San Carlos. The

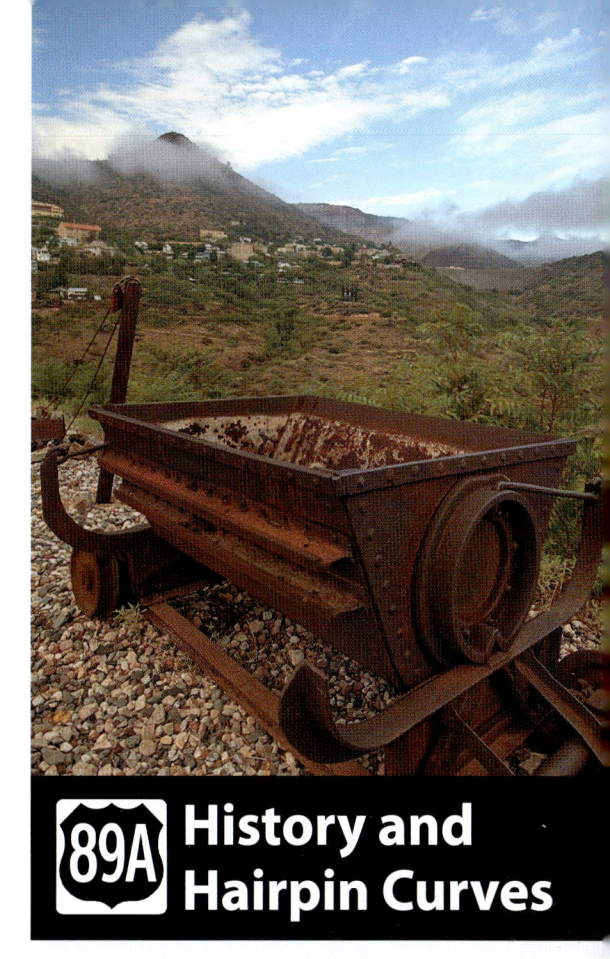

89A History and Hairpin Curves

The former U.S. 89A–the A stood for alternate–offers motorists a scenic back road from Prescott to Flagstaff. The road winds around Mingus Mountain and into the historic town of Jerome (above), where miners once extracted over $1 billion in gold and other minerals. In 1903, Jerome was labeled as "the wildest town in the West" by the *New York Sun*. Now a National Historic Landmark and artist colony, Jerome attracts a steady stream of tourists to its hairpin-turn streets.

Descending into Verde Valley, the highway passes Tuzigoot National Monument, another gem in Arizona's collection of Sinaguan archaeological sites (see Wupatki National Monument in Chapter 4). Then Sedona's red rocks come into view. Sedona is perhaps best known for its New Age "vortices" among its formations.

From Sedona, the road parallels Oak Creek and passes local favorite Slide Rock State Park. More winding turns in the canyon gorge lead to Flagstaff. Decommissioned in 1992, along with Highway 89 south of Flagstaff, U.S. 89A is now numbered Arizona 89A.

US Highway 89: Arizona ★ 37

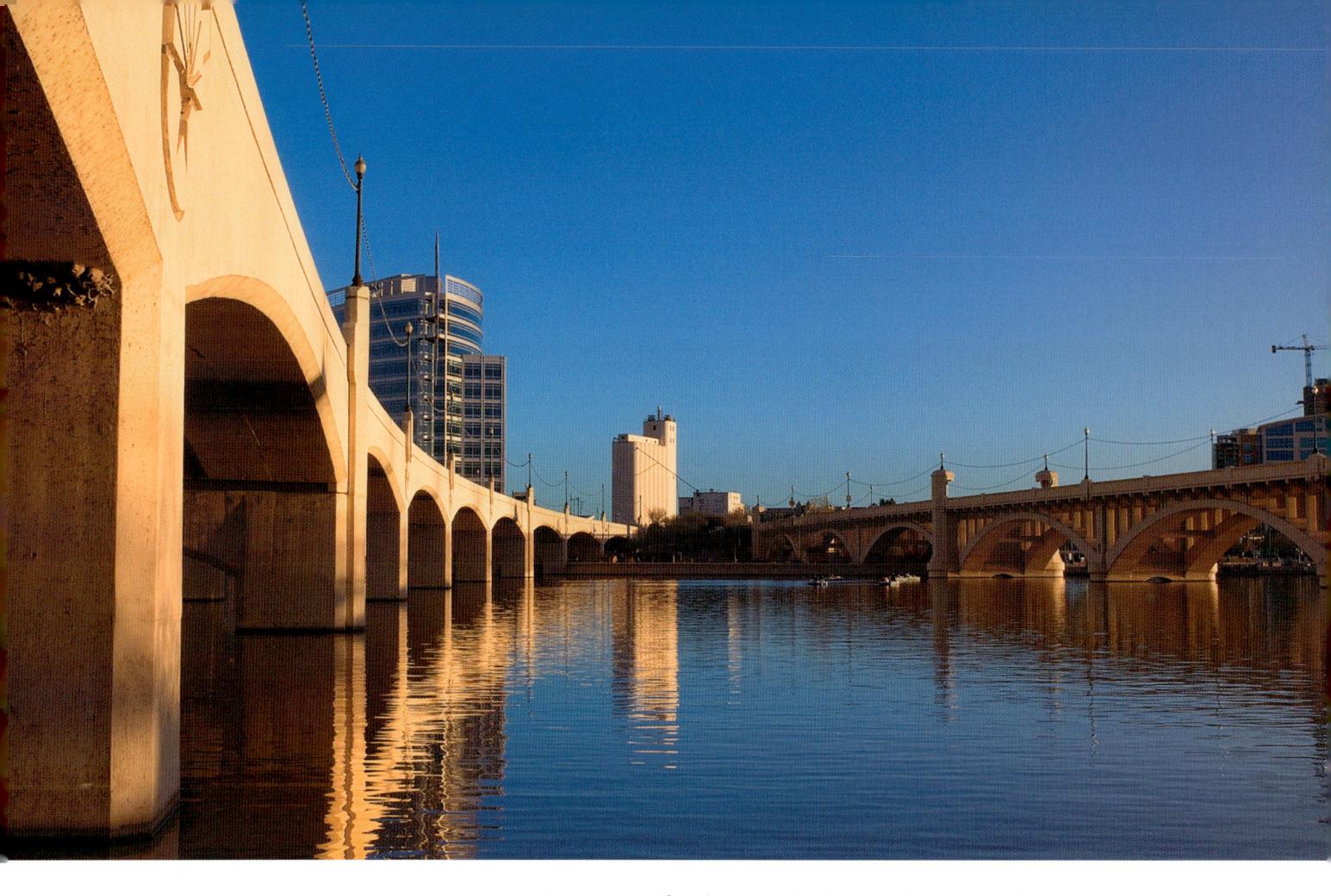

LIGHT SHOW: The newest bridge over the Salt River (opposite) carries the Phoenix metropolitan area's light rail trains. A moving pattern of colored lights sweeps across the span paralleling the Mill Avenue bridges.

MILL AVENUE BRIDGES: Despite upsteam dams, the Salt River is occasionally dangerous as tremendous flash floods can fill its banks a quarter mile across. First spanned in 1911, the original bridge was replaced with a stronger structure on the right (above), completed in 1931. During record floods of 1980, the bridge was one of the few passable routes over the river. The bridge on the left was built in 1994.

Yavapai suffered more deaths on the 150-mile march, then worked to irrigate new fields, ultimately losing that land to coal-mining and damming projects.

By 1901, most of the tribe had left San Carlos. Reservations were ultimately established for three of the four traditional subtribes, including one in 1935 at the abandoned Fort Whipple in Prescott (likely the group referenced in the FWA guide book). With less than 1,400 acres, but those lands centered in one of Arizona's fastest growing communities, the Prescott Yavapai have leveraged their tribal assets through real estate development that includes a hotel/casino complex on a bluff overlooking Highway 89.

The Smoki People

As tribal people like the Yavapai were struggling to regain their lands, or even to win voting rights as American citizens, "pot-hunting" became a popular hobby in the 1920s. Anglos collected Indian art and artifacts while lamenting "disappearing" native cultures.

In 1921, Prescottians formed a civic club, the Smoki (pronounced smoke-eye) People, to stage a fund-raiser for the rodeo. The performance turned into an annual event, and the society later built a museum and clubhouse for their artifact collections.

The Smoki People performed their interpretations of Indian ceremonials in full costume, complete with a Hopi Snake Dance

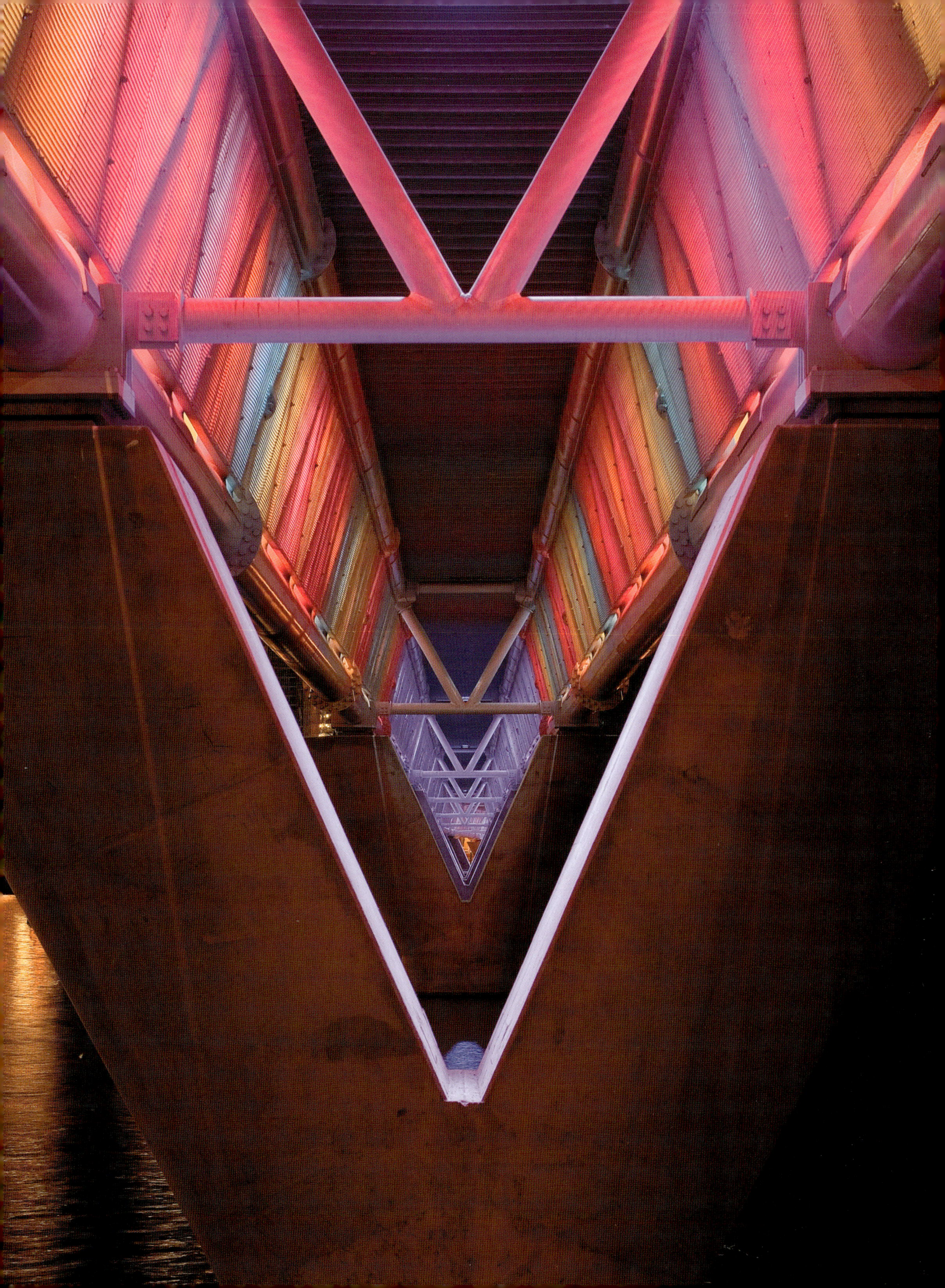

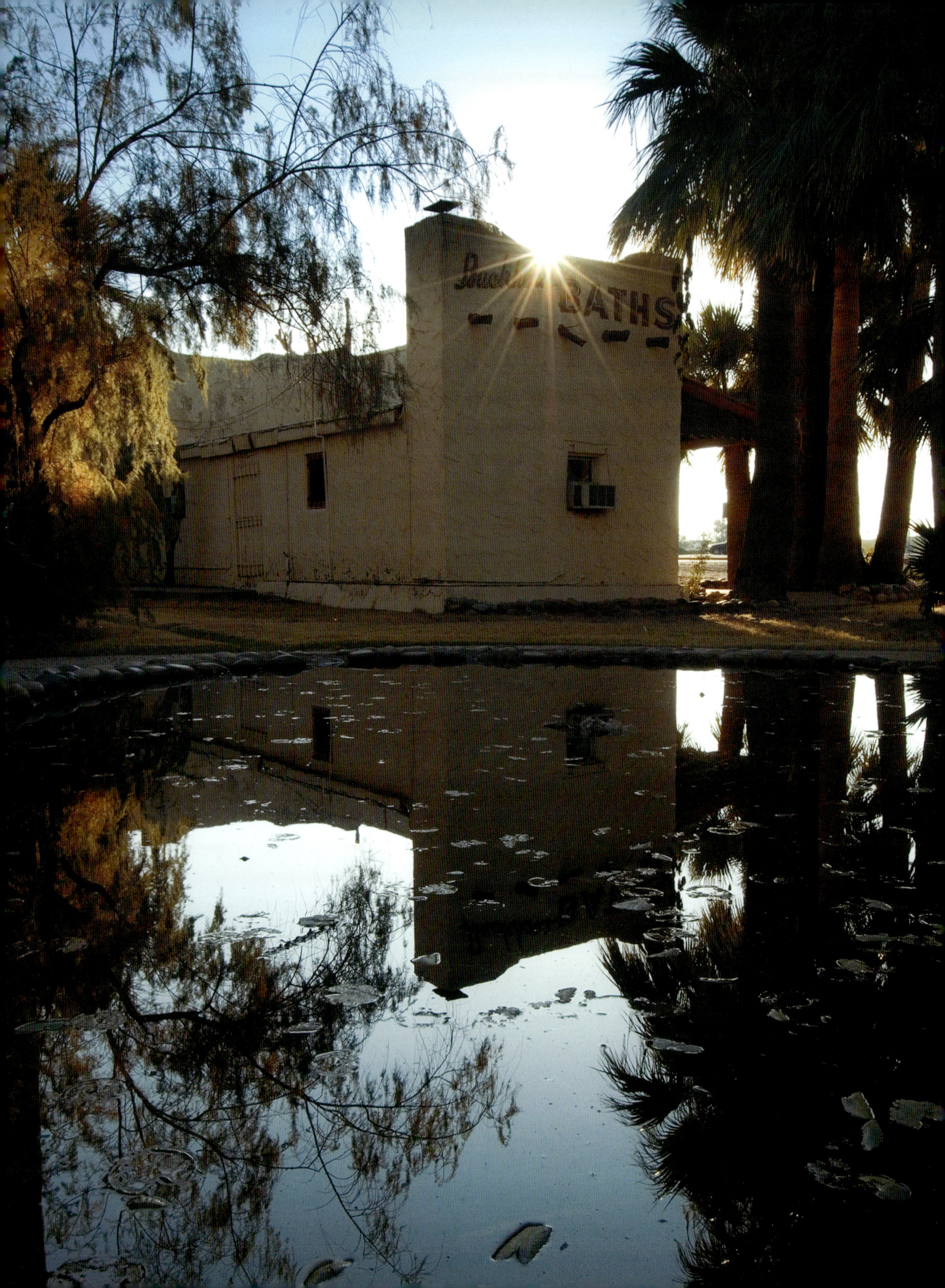
BATHS

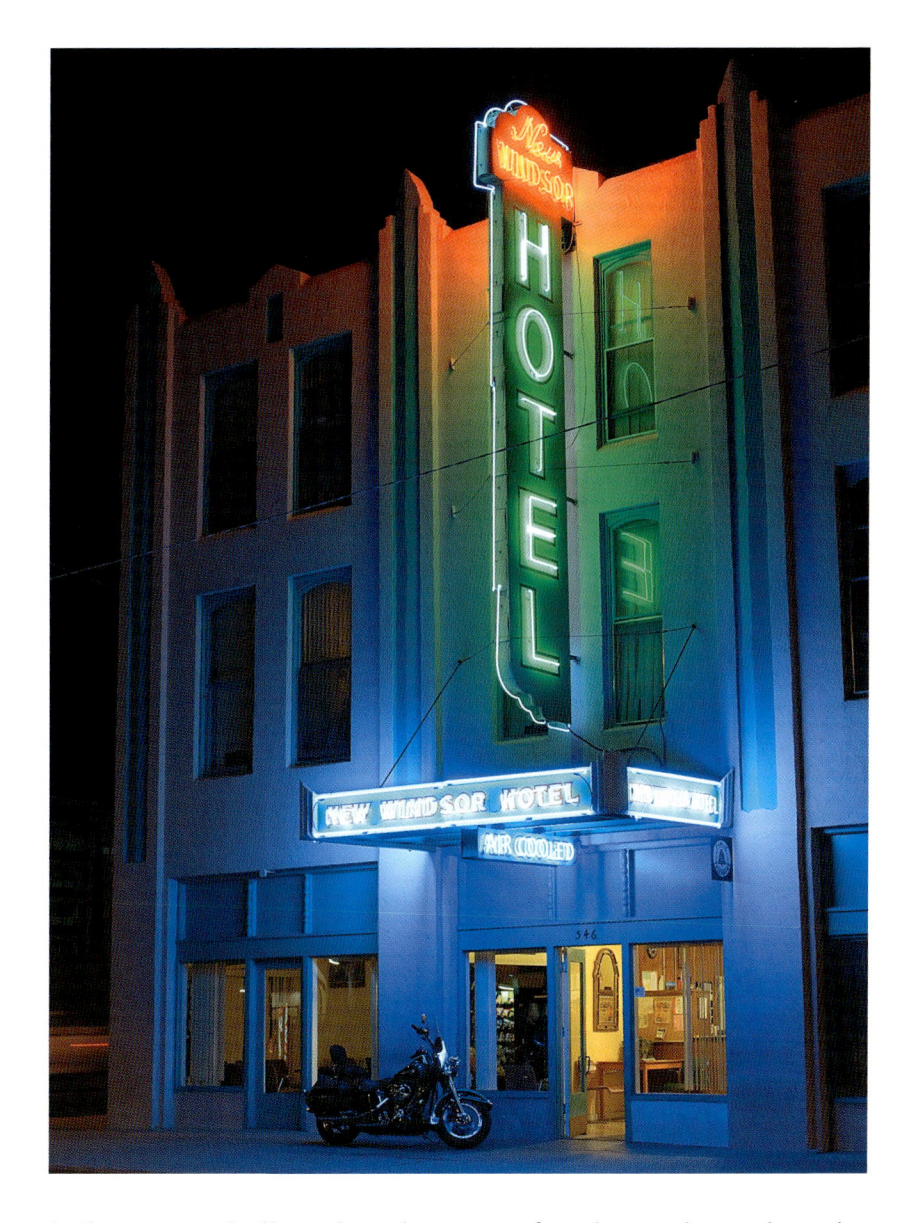

BUCKHORN BATHS: The Buckhorn Baths (opposite) welcomed travelers along U.S. 89 for over 60 years. Ted and Alice Sliger built the mineral baths, taxidermy museum and motel units along Arizona's major connecting route between Tucson and Phoenix. From the late 1940s through the early 1970s, the New York Giants baseball team stayed at the baths for Cactus League spring training. Ted died in 1984; Alice continued to run the resort into her 90s. The property will likely be demolished to make way for another big-box store.

NEW WINDSOR HOTEL: Built in 1893, the New Windsor (left) now offers long-term housing to the Phoenix needy.

(substituting bull snakes, however, for the traditional rattlesnakes). Tattoos marked status in the club; at its peak, the society's membership included a remarkably egalitarian representation of Prescott's Anglo community. The Smoki leaders suggested they were perpetuating the rituals of the Southwest; Hopi leaders, attending the event for the first time in 1990, saw otherwise and objected. In the face of declining membership and changing cultural values, the Smokis halted the performances. Museum curators have since installed a history exhibit of the Smoki People, which incorporates interviews with dance participants and Hopi representatives. Today, the reinvention of the Smoki Museum continues: it now presents traditional and emerging native artists alongside its original collections.

Growth and Decommissioning

Phoenix's transformation from a regional hub to the nation's fifth largest city began during World War II, when defense industries

ROUGH RIDER: Sculptor Solon Borglum specialized in western bronzes; *Rough Rider* (right) is considered his finest work. Solon originally wanted to be a rancher. Only after years of cowboying did he follow his brother Gutzon (Mt. Rushmore's sculptor) to study art. The Arizona Territory commissioned this statue to honor Captain William "Buckey" O'Neil, one of its most prominent citizens before he resigned as mayor of Prescott to join Theodore Roosevelt's Rough Riders. O'Neil died in action in Cuba in 1898. The statue was unveiled in 1907 on the plaza of the Yavapai County Courthouse. Prescott decorates the Courthouse each year as part of its tradition as "Arizona's Christmas City."

GRANITE DELLS: North of Prescott, Highway 89 twists through an outcropping of ancient, Precambrian granite, weathered into striking rounded forms. The man-made reservoir at Watson Lake Park (opposite) is a popular summer recreation destination.

relocated from Los Angeles to avoid Japanese attack. The post-war trend of migration to the Sun Belt states, the wide-spread adoption of air conditioning, and the G.I. Bill, which enabled home-ownership for many veterans, spurred suburban development along Arizona's primary highways, particularly Highway 89 from Mesa to Glendale.

West of Glendale on Highway 89, Arizona real estate contractor and part-owner of the Yankees baseball team, Del Webb, built the first active senior housing development in the Sun Belt states. At the 1960 grand opening, more than 100,000 people toured Sun City's model homes, and Webb sold 237 units in three days. By promoting an "active adult lifestyle" to a post-war generation of retirees, Webb sold plenty of real estate. In 1978, the development expanded to Sun City West and the twin communities now anchor one of Arizona's fastest growing areas.

Modest tourist camps and trailer courts that dotted Arizona's first highways were gradually transformed into residential parks, creating a completely new lifestyle for middle-class seniors. Companies like Airstream offered travel trailers especially for retired couples as early as the mid-1930s. Campgrounds provided electrical and water connections and "snowbirds" settled into winter quarters along Highway 89, particularly in the Apache Junction area. Seasonal migrants boost Arizona's winter population by 250,000 or more, with more than half residing in mobile home and trailer parks. In 2000, more than 80,000 part-timers stayed in parks in the Phoenix area and the 35,000 snowbirds who return to Apache Junction nearly double the town's summer population.

Highway traffic helped sustain a string of smaller Arizona towns until the 1950s construction of the interstate system threatened to bypass them altogether. In Wickenburg, the intersection of U.S. 60 and U.S. 89 was claimed to be the busiest corner in America (although a traffic light was not installed there until 1987). Wickenburg was finally bypassed by the 1973 opening of the Brenda cut-off on Interstate 10. Phoenix's political machinations delayed final completion of I-10 through the metroplex until 1990.

The familiar black and white shield signs came down when U.S. 89 south of Flagstaff was decommissioned in 1992. Absorbed as segments in Arizona's state highway system, old Highway 89 still links and invigorates the communities it serves. Mesa volunteers lead winter season art tours along dozens of sculptures on Main Street. Arizona State University's new downtown Phoenix campus is propelling redevelopment in the Van Buren Street district. Prescott starts its Whisky Row Marathon on the town plaza.

Modernized and reinvented to serve a growing state, only glimpses of the old highway remain, but on a few two-lane stretches, like from Oracle to Florence or Prescott to Ashfork, today's motorists can still experience what it might have been like to travel Arizona's very first highway.

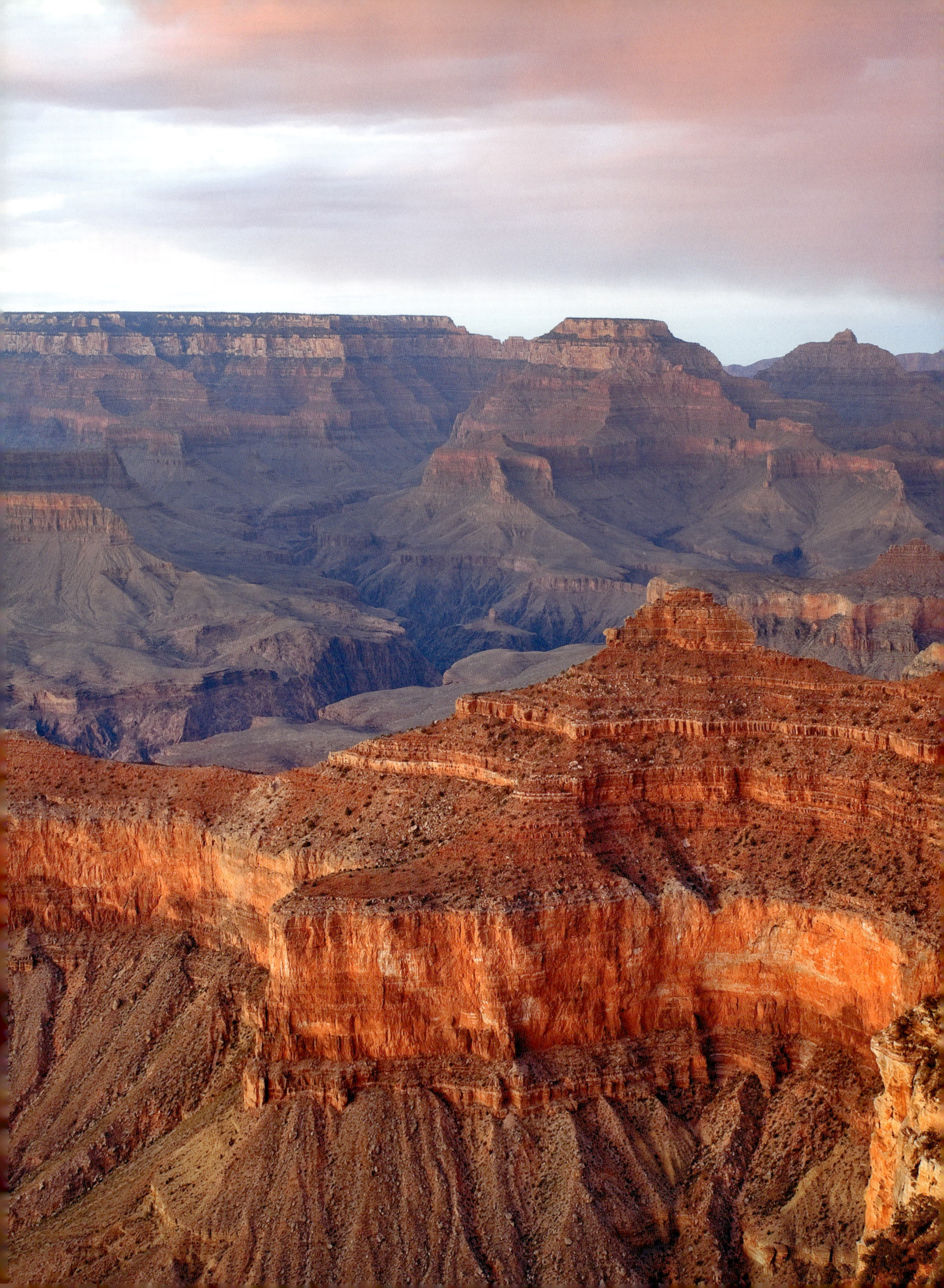

The Honeymoon Trail
★ ★ ★ Flagstaff to Page, Arizona ★ ★ ★ ★ ★ ★ ★ ★ ★

From Tucson to Flagstaff, motorists in 1925 drove Arizona's most modern highway. Northbound travelers, however, were out of luck beyond Flagstaff. The Coconino County road to the Utah border was marked as "unimproved" on the official state map. It was so bad, in fact, that Grand Canyon superintendents urged motorists to detour hundreds of miles through Las Vegas to visit the North Rim.

Four years later, not one mile northward had been paved, but U.S. 89 from Nogales to Fredonia appeared on the official state map, part of the federal government cost-sharing program for a primary highway network. Arizona, focused instead on luring transcontinental automobile traffic, would take another decade to finish the highway across the Colorado Plateau.

With every mile of concrete, the federal highways changed the economic landscape for capturing tourism dollars. By the end of the 1920s, three out of four families owned a car and middle-class Americans were driving them to their national parks. Visitation to Grand Canyon National Park tripled in 10 years, inspired by popular western writers, films and well-publicized visits by Buffalo Bill Cody and President Theodore Roosevelt.

The explosion of automobile traffic in the 1920s challenged the Grand Canyon National Park officials beyond the need to simply improve park roads. The typical railway-arriving tourist booked a complete package tour from the Atchison, Topeka & Santa Fe Railway concessionaires. The new motoring public might not be able to afford Fred Harvey's deluxe accommodations at the El Tovar Hotel, but they could buy gasoline and camping outfits. Park rangers had to adapt to visitors who showed up without warning and simply pitched their tents in the middle of the village. Fred Harvey built a garage; the National Park Service opened free campgrounds with amenities like running water, flush toilets, stores and firewood.

SUNSET FROM YAVAPAI POINT: Grand Canyon National Park (opposite)

DESERT WATCHTOWER: Mary Colter's architecture set the tone for Fred Harvey's tourism empire in the Southwest. She designed the 1933 Watchtower (above) in Grand Canyon National Park to look like an Anasazi structure, specifying that the cut faces of each stone be turned inward toward the supporting steel structure so that only naturally weathered stone surfaces are visible.

US HIGHWAY 89: ARIZONA ★ 45

After 80 years of interstate road programs, U.S. 89 remains Arizona's only northbound highway. A second bridge now crosses the mighty Colorado River, but traffic still slows to 25 miles per hour on either two-lane span. This still-lonely stretch of Highway 89 recaptures an earlier era of motoring, as it gently ascends to the ponderosa-topped mesa at Ashfork, crests the San Francisco Peaks near Flagstaff and rolls across the red-rock country of the Colorado Plateau.

Ancient Travelers

Native peopled have inhabited the Colorado Plateau for millennia. More than 4,000 years ago, hunter-gatherers concealed split-twig figurines of bighorn sheep or deer in some of the most inaccessible caves in the Grand Canyon. Later, Anasazi farmers built granaries high above the Colorado River to protect their harvest from rodents and floods. The Hopi people still maintain their traditional right to collect salt from mines near the confluence with the Little Colorado River within Grand Canyon National Park.

Scientists classify civilizations by their technologies and lifeways, but archeological fragments are difficult to gather into the song of a people. The Sinaguan ruins of Wupatki National Monument whisper a refrain

46 ✶ The Honeymoon Trail

of early life on the Colorado Plateau. The stone walls no longer echo with shouts of children hauling water in their mothers' hand-made clay vessels, the rhythmic beats of wood-chopping and corn-grinding, the bustle of readying an expedition to harvest piñon nuts, or the cheers of a crowd at the meso-American style ballcourt.

Nearly 1,000 years ago, Sunset Crater erupted for the first time, becoming the youngest member of the San Francisco Peaks. As nearby Sinaguans moved away from falling ash and lava bombs, strangers journeyed long distances to learn the meaning of the plume, which would have been visible from the mountaintops at Durango, Colorado, and Palm Springs, California. Under the smoking cider cone, a short-lived but culturally rich community of pueblos emerged.

Early archeologists offered explanations like drought, warfare and religious exodus to explain the mystery of the depopulation of the Sinaguan pueblos by the 14th century. Native tradition, on the other hand, offers a succinct answer. The Sinaguans didn't disappear, rather they migrated to larger pueblos to the north and are revered today by their descendants in several Hopi clans.

Grand Canyon: Buttes as Tall as Mountain Ranges
The Colorado Plateau stretches from Arizona to Colorado, in 130,000 square miles of orderly sedimentary formations. For 600 million

LOMAKI RUIN: The Sinaguan people built these dwellings above the western edge of the Painted Desert in what is now Wupatki National Monument. The volcanic range of the nearby San Francisco Peaks has erupted as recently as AD 1100. At its peak, the pueblo community grew to about 2,000. (opposite)

ANCIENT BALLCOURT: The ballcourt at Wupatki National Monument was excavated and restored in 1965. (below)

WINDOW ONTO WINTER: The population of Sinaguan people in the Walnut Canyon National Monument area grew after the eruption of Sunset Crater Volcano. Unlike their neighbors at Wupatki, they lived in cliff dwellings, unique in northern Sinaguan culture. (above)

SUNSET CRATER VOLCANO NATIONAL MONUMENT: Outrage over a Hollywood film crew's plans to dynamite Sunset Crater resulted in public support to create a national monument to protect it in 1930. (opposite)

years, this section of the earth's crust has uniquely been spared reshaping by normal tectonic plate activity.

The depositions of the Colorado Plateau have fractured into sub-units—the Coconino, Kaibab and more plateaus that the highway will cross in Utah. These plateaus have shifted relative vertical positions but remain intact; rivers cutting through the plateaus reveal the same geologic progression for hundreds of miles, although one layer may be displaced upward several thousand feet.

Ponderosa pines blanket the Coconino Plateau, forming the largest unbroken pine forest in North America. At the brink of the Grand Canyon, the forest gives way to a vastness of light and air as the earth falls away at one's feet. Buttes and pinnacles spread out in a panorama of color and texture. The distance to the North Rim averages eleven miles, and the buttes themselves are as tall as entire mountain ranges in the eastern U.S. The Colorado River is as much as a mile below the rim, yet on a still morning it is possible to hear the rapids roar below Lipan Point on the South Rim.

The seeming paradox of the Grand Canyon's spectacular demonstration of erosive power is that the South Rim is so arid. At 7,000 feet, the Coconino Plateau receives 24 inches of moisture, but its limestone cap quickly absorbs most of the runoff, which percolates

48 ★ THE HONEYMOON TRAIL

downward until it emerges as springs 2,000 feet below the mesa top. Only two major tributaries enter from the south. The Kaibab Plateau's higher elevation results in more precipitation and it slants toward the river. These factors shaped the vista: the north canyon walls expose a broad sweep of temples and promontories between side canyons formed by the river's tributaries.

The Grand Canyon chasm is relatively new: continental plate movements from only about 30 million years ago realigned North American drainage patterns to create the Colorado River. Enlarged by melting glaciers, the river worked quickly, eroding through as much as 6,000 feet of sediment to create the Grand Canyon of today.

The Day of the Condors
Rafting guide John Toner, a veteran of 97 descents of the Grand Canyon, was piloting another expedition when he saw a condor in 1998. Soaring 1,000 feet above the river, the huge size and flight pattern indicated it was a bird he had never seen before. He grabbed his binoculars to confirm the identification, the first he'd seen in the three years since the raptors had been reintroduced to the wild.

Condors are known to loaf near the release site beneath the Vermilion Cliffs, and even to roost in Marble Canyon near the highway bridge, but they aren't always easy to find.

One December day, a snowstorm was clearing at the South Rim of the Grand Canyon. Wisps of clouds formed below the rim and dissipated as the air currents wafted them out of the canyon. Ravens were on the move. Ragged flocks landed just below the rim to pick through the snow on the talus. One flock numbered over two hundred ravens, but no condors soared that day.

As the sun heats the south-facing walls of the canyon, convective winds provide lift that raptors use to efficiently cover vast feeding territories. Unlike songbirds, larger raptors roost until the thermals develop, often late in the morning. When they launch, they spiral upward on a rising current, then descend in a shallow glide to search for prey, carrion or another thermal lift. That condor strategy fails if the weather doesn't cooperate, like one spring morning when a weather system had settled cold air on the Colorado Plateau. Only feet above the landmark El Tovar Hotel, five condors circled–the birds couldn't find a thermal in the cold, still air.

On the esplanade between the hotel and the canyon edge trail, condors zoomed by like jets on patrol, some below in the canyon, others barely clearing the trees as they searched for rising air. They cruised by for hours, often passing so close that the numbers on their shoulder tags could be read without binoculars.

A strolling mendicant naturalist of a ranger, who could have been the ghost of John Muir except for his uniform, told visitors that a condor pair had just hatched an egg below Maricopa Point along Hermits Rest Drive. Condors flew past the Corn Pollen Dancers as they performed outside the Hopi House. Not until mid-afternoon did the air warm up enough to build up thermals, and about that time the condors vanished for the day.

Some scientists describe condors as a living relic of the age of gigantic mammals, having evolved as carrion feeders of mastodons and giant sloths. As their diet shifted to elk and other game, the condors were reduced to perhaps a few hundred individuals by the time the arriving European settlers (prejudiced against the vulture on principle) shot them indiscriminately. Some prospectors even used their quills as containers for gold dust. The El Tovar portico bears an inscription above the hotel entry, "Dreams of Mountains as in their sleep, they brood on things eternal." Even if mountains were eternal, the condors are not. Only because of an unprecedented decision to take the last of the wild population into a captive breeding program are condors flying over the Grand Canyon today. It is a fool's errand

BRIGHT ANGEL LODGE: The Santa Fe Railway built the visitor infrastructure for the South Rim of the Grand Canyon, including the famous El Tovar Hotel. Union Pacific Railway had the concession for the national parks of the Grand Circle: Zion, Bryce and the North Rim. With its nearest depot more than 100 miles away, the Union Pacific built properties, like Bright Angel Lodge (below), at a more modest scale.

RISING MISTS: A winter storm lifts from the South Rim of the Grand Canyon (opposite, above).

CALIFORNIA CONDOR: The last 22 wild California condors were captured for a last-ditch breeding program in 1987; six immature condors were reintroduced in 1996 to the ecosystem in the Vermilion Cliffs area. Today, nearly 60 condors (opposite, below) soar over the Grand Canyon area, and a pair successfully fledged the first wild-born chick in 2003.

perhaps, in evolutionary time scales, but why not? The sight of a condor rising out of the void of the Grand Canyon delights lucky park visitors and symbolizes the ongoing efforts to preserve the Grand Canyon itself.

Fire and Fireworks on the Plateau

In 1917, a motoring trip to Williams wasn't easy; the local paper lamented that drivers often chose to ship their cars from Flagstaff by train to avoid damage from bad roads. U.S. Highway 66 eventually connected the two, with 50 miles of the "mother road" co-numbered with Highway 89 from Ashfork to Flagstaff. Williams was the last Route 66 town to be bypassed by Interstate 40, in 1984.

Nostalgia for Route 66 has become a profitable draw for Williams, as has the revival of the Grand Canyon Railway, with its renovated depot in the heart of town. Tourists now drive long distances to ride the train into the park, an ironic turn of events considering that the popularity of the automobile hastened the demise of passenger railway travel.

Usually, the Fourth of July is a bit early for the shift in weather

FOURTH OF JULY ON ROUTE 66: Classic car clubs converge each summer for the Williams Fourth of July parade (opposite) along Route 66, also the historic route of Highway 89.

ANTIQUE GAS PUMP: on the historic route of U.S. 66/89 in Williams (left)

RETRO 66 SIGNAGE: Williams has posted the historic Route 66 through their downtown with signs patterned after the traditional shield design. (above)

patterns that brings tropical moisture from the Baja California coast to Arizona. In 2007, any relief from the record heat and match-dry conditions would have been welcomed by the entire state of Arizona. Even the high altitude communities around Flagstaff were sweltering and the risk of forest fires was already extraordinarily high. Citing the fire danger, Flagstaff's officialdom cancelled the city fireworks display, to the dismay of youth groups stuck with pre-paid fund-raiser goodies and no place to sell them. Down the highway, the town of Williams insisted that their safety plan was adequate and invited Flagstaff's citizens to their celebration.

Marching along the historic Route 66, Williams' Fourth of July parade starred local veterans, scouts, politicians and Yavapai tribal members (earlier in the day, the Flagstaff parade honored the last of the World War II Navajo Code Talker veterans). Classic cars of every vintage rolled past, a 1970s muscle car growling behind a pristine Model T. A cherry red motor trike, newly restored and decorated with toys from a Williams second-hand shop, was a crowd favorite: Santa had donned a red T-shirt and joined the parade.

Arizona doesn't have any use for daylight savings time–days are

DOWNTOWNER: Scaffolding elevates several Flagstaff hotel and motel signs. (above)

HOTEL MONTE VISTA: The landmark Hotel Monte Vista (right) hosted numerous Hollywood stars during the 1940s and 50s. Scenes from the movie *Casablanca* were filmed in one of the hotel's rooms.

SMOKE BREAK: The transcontinental railway reached Flagstaff in 1882. Railways brought cattlemen, including five brothers from Cincinnati, Ohio. The Babbitts launched their ranching enterprise, the CO Bar, in 1886. Almost immediately, they branched out into other businesses, such as Flagstaff's first soda fountain, a lumberyard that developed into a chain of department stores, and an ice plant. In 1905, their meatpacking company sponsored a parade float graced by a "sausage queen." Today, Northern Arizona University has replaced the railway, ranching and timber industries as Flagstaff's top employer. The downtown has a vibrant college-town atmosphere. (opposite)

long enough when temperatures exceed 100 degrees for months at a time. The evening was still hot when the first fireworks flashed across the Williams sky. Even though the launch site had been relocated twice leading up to July 4th and firefighters were immediately at hand, within five minutes the show was stopped because falling debris touched off a wildfire. The column of flames shot up, visible to the line of traffic streaming along the interstate toward Flagstaff.

The rivalry between Flagstaff and Williams dates back to the 1891 election deciding the location of the county seat (Flagstaff won, 419 votes to 97). So it wasn't surprising that in the local newspaper report of the fire, Flagstaff politicians congratulated themselves on their good judgment or that Williams officials defended their preparedness for the fire. It seems, like a forest fire in a drought, town rivalries can flare up with the least bit of spark.

Mile Markers

Although Highway 89 was decommissioned south of Flagstaff in 1992, the mile marker posts were not renumbered, so the official route northward begins at mile marker (MM) 418, in the middle of a perpetual construction zone at the Interstate 40/U.S. 89 interchange. Beyond the traffic lights that signal another wave of suburban sprawl, a 1940 guide to Arizona highways describes the route to Bitter Springs as well as (if not better than) any contemporary guidebook.

Cresting the pass through the San Francisco Peaks, as the radio loses reception from the megapower Spanglish station in Phoenix, the highway cuts a straight swath through the airy ponderosa pine forest. At the horizon, the black lanes converge into the coral and ochre tones of the western edge of the Painted Desert.

A huge painting by cowboy artist Bill Owen announces the annual colt sale at the historic Babbitt Ranches. Mostly, it is the absence of

GHOSTLY GUARDIANS: This sculpture rests beside the highway on the margin of Wupatki National Monument. (above)

HORSESHOE BEND: Sinuous curves of the Colorado River near Page (opposite)

billboards and fast food signs that leaves room to notice the scenery: piñon and cedar woodlands, sagebrush and rabbitbrush, with its yellow October blooms. Metal towers, carrying power from the twin engines of the Glen Canyon Dam and the Navajo Generating Station, look like a column of mythical giants striding across the desert.

Soon the radio will crackle again as the Tuba City station comes into range. Navajo-accented disc jockeys play eclectic rock-and-roll mixes and bilingual community announcements, unless preempted by a high school basketball game. The western end of the Navajo nation is more cattle country than the sheep-raising land to the east. A few traditional hogans nestle alongside western-style houses set far back from the road, with beautiful horses in corrals.

No special geological training is required to appreciate the landscape unfurling at highway speed. Late afternoon light accentuates the badlands around milemarker 485; at midmorning, massive boulders stand in relief from the base of Echo Cliffs. Under a blue May sky, orange globe mallow blossoms seem to pull their brilliant pigments right out of the coral-colored soil.

Highway 89 divides at Bitter Springs. Long after John Wesley Powell's descent of the Colorado River, its canyons still present trav-

56 ★ THE HONEYMOON TRAIL

elers with a formidable obstacle. For 750 miles there are only seven possible land crossings–and the Highway 89 story crosses two of them, less than 20 river miles apart.

Crossing the Colorado

Sharlot Hall wrote one of the earliest travel guides to the Colorado Plateau region. Hall never married, but ran her aging parents' ranch near Prescott while working as a contributor and editor for a Los Angeles magazine. A political appointee as Arizona's territorial historian, Hall wrote about her remarkable trip to the Kaibab Plateau and Arizona Strip in 1911, in which she and a hired guide traveled more than 1,000 miles by wagon to collect first-person pioneer histories.

Hall followed a rough but well-established route known as the Honeymoon Trail because of its extensive use by Mormon settlers. Certain sacred rites of The Church of Jesus Christ of Latter-day Saints were (and are) reserved for temples. Until the LDS temple in Mesa was dedicated in 1927, the nearest one to the Arizona settlements was in St. George, Utah. Couples married in a civil ceremony in their communities and, as soon as finances and farming duties would allow, undertook a nearly weeklong journey to St. George to solemnize their vows. Hall noted that early Mormon travelers had planted Lombardy poplars to mark the trail. Even today, mixed in with the closely related native

89 Wupatki's first rangers

No housing was provided for the first rangers at Wupatki National Monument. Instead Jimmie Brewer and his wife Sallie resided in the Wupatki pueblo itself. The next ranger, Davy Jones, installed a propane refrigerator–electricity arrived in 1947. His wife Corky Jones wrote a book, *Letters from Wupatki*, about life among the ruins.

MARBLE CANYON: Matching old and new bridges (right) span Marble Canyon six miles below Lee's Ferry. The nearest bridge was set in place in 1995; the original (1929) bridge is now open to foot traffic.

ANTELOPE CANYON: Guide Nate Tsosie plays a native flute in Antelope Canyon (opposite) near Page. Navajo Sandstone erodes into narrow slot canyons. During monsoon season, flash floods can inundate the canyon with dangerous walls of rolling mud, rock and debris. As a Navajo Tribal Park, Antelope Canyon's spectacular formations can be visited only with a licensed guide.

ORANGE GLOBE MALLOW (below)

cottonwoods, a few columnar descendants of those green beacons grow along the route.

At highway speeds, the significance of bridges in this arid land is hard to appreciate. Not so when Hall forded the Little Colorado River, trusting her guide not to lose their wagon in quicksand. In her book, she reported that a new bridge at Cameron soon would alleviate that risky crossing. The one-lane suspension bridge installed in 1911 is still there next to Highway 89, repurposed to support a fuel pipeline across the still-treacherous Little Colorado river.

The Navajo Bridge, opened to traffic in 1929, eliminated the worst danger on the highway: the Lee's Ferry crossing. Sandwiched between sheer vertical cliffs, it was barely possible to construct dugways down to the river from the surrounding plateaus. Sharlot Hall wrote, "The

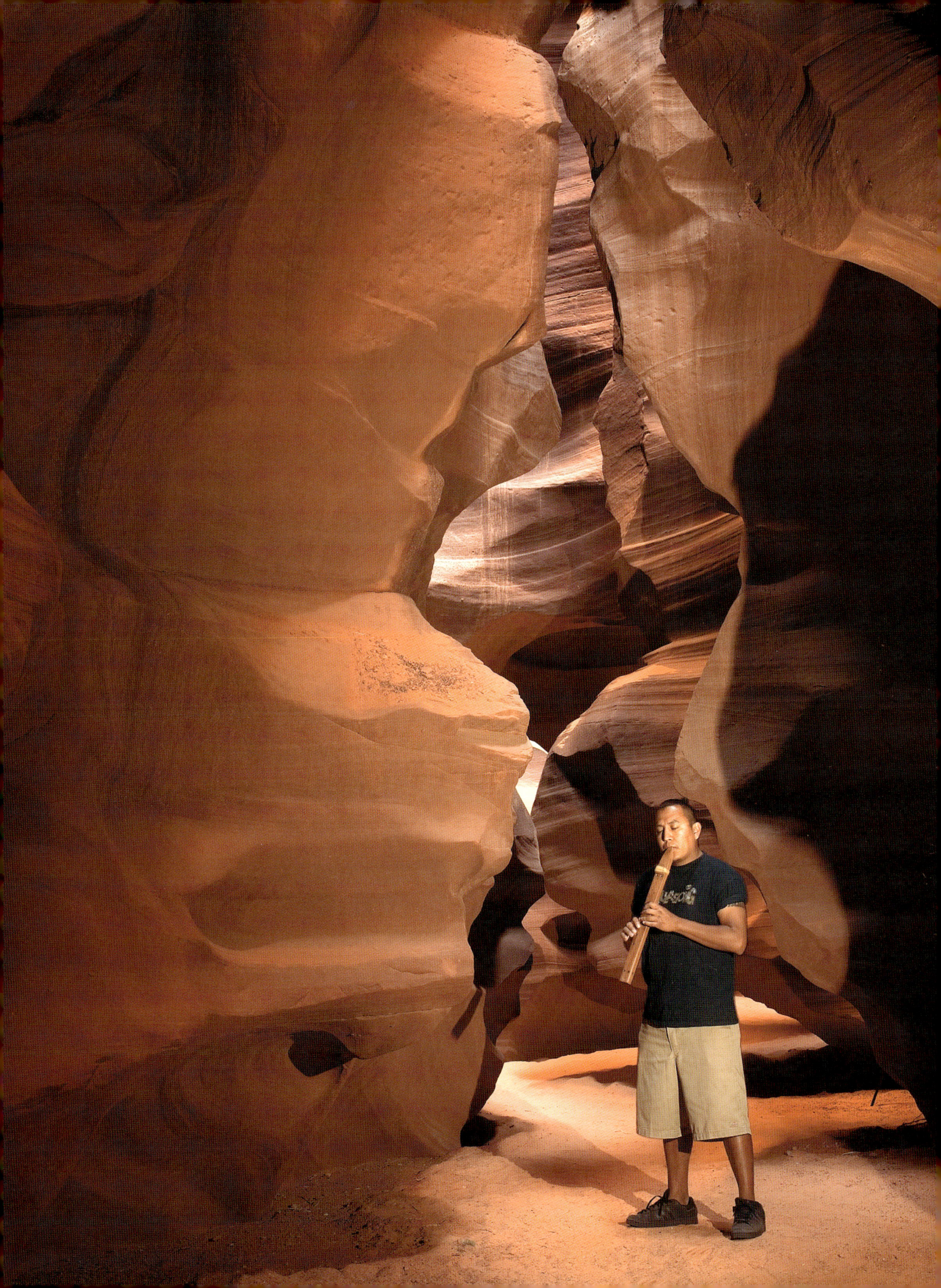

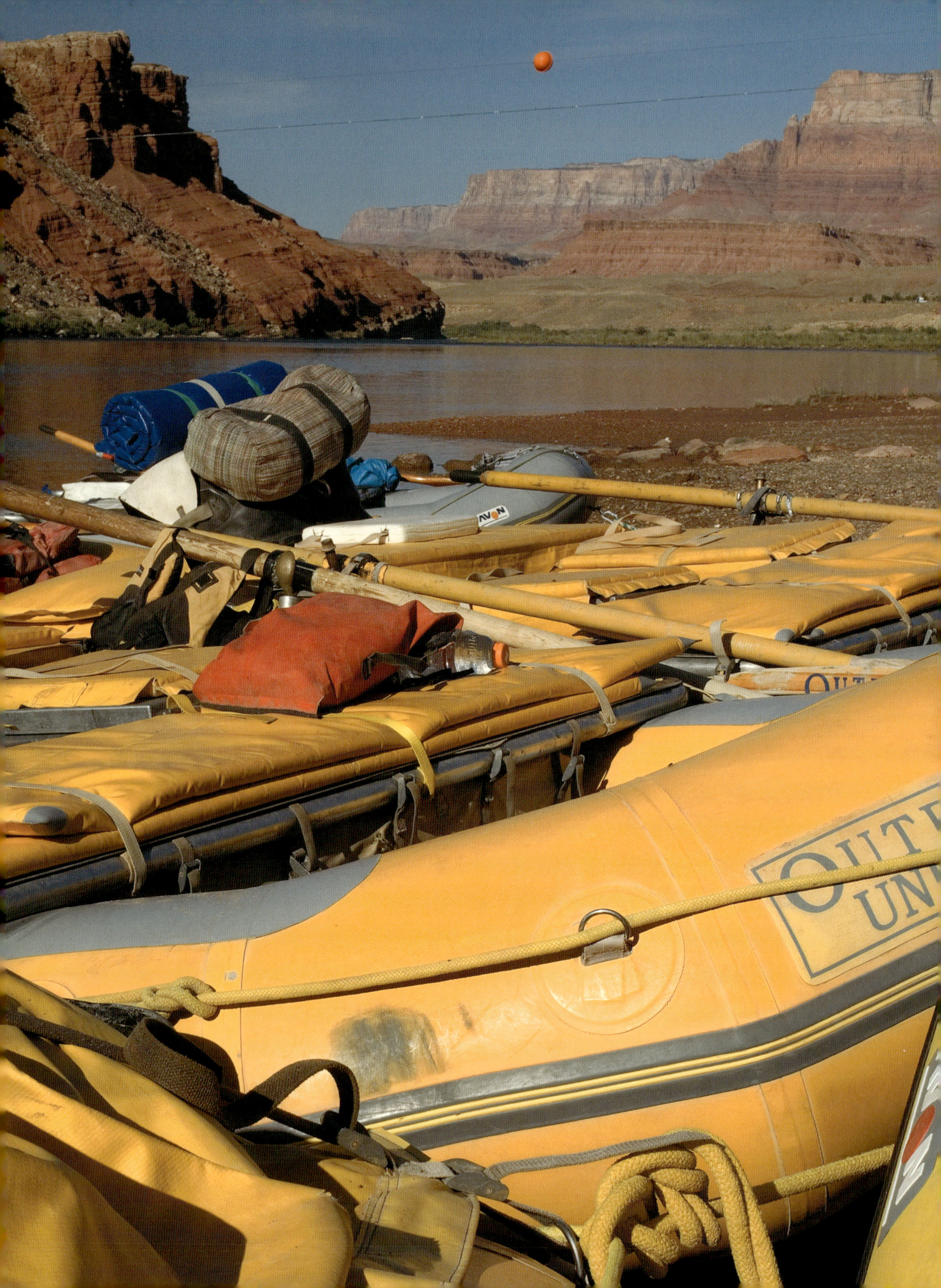
AVON
OUTE
UN

road looked as if it had been cut out of the red clay mountains with a pocket knife; sometimes it hung out over the river so we seemed sliding into the muddy current and again the cliffs above hung over till one grew dizzy to look."

No one could cross the Colorado River at the height of spring runoff when 100,000 cubic feet of water blasted by each second. In drought years, the river could be waded; some travelers would risk a crossing on foot if the winter ice was thick. Eleven people lost their lives in the nearly 60 years of ferry service, which closed for good in 1928 when the boat capsized, washing away a Model T and drowning three passengers.

Six miles downstream, Navajo Bridge rises 467 feet above the river, the world's highest highway span when it was built. The bridge formed an essential link for the residents of the Arizona Strip, isolated from the rest of the state, including their county seat in Flagstaff. In 1995, vehicular traffic shifted to a wider bridge installed a few yards to the south. The old structure remains open to foot traffic, serving visitors from an interpretive center hosted by the Glen Canyon National Recreation Area.

For nearly 30 years, all north-south traffic between Moab and Las Vegas funneled across the two lanes of Navajo Bridge and over the

LEE'S FERRY: Commercial outfitters and private parties rig rafts at Lee's Ferry before running the Colorado River's 280 miles to Lake Mead. (opposite)

GLEN CANYON BRIDGE: Lights from semi-trucks and passenger cars streak across the Glen Canyon Bridge beneath a holiday greeting from the Glen Canyon Dam workers. (above)

VERMILION CLIFFS: The original Highway 89, now U.S. 89A, parallels the Vermilion Cliffs before climbing onto the Kaibab Plateau. (following pages)

snowy Kaibab Plateau. Then, in 1956, on a secluded corner of the Navajo reservation about 15 miles upstream, President Dwight Eisenhower pushed a remote control in the White House to trigger the first construction blast for the Glen Canyon Dam.

Without a new bridge over the Colorado River, getting to the opposite side of the job site required a nearly 200-mile drive. The Glen Canyon Bridge, 700 feet above the river, was a welcome replacement for the swinging footbridge that dam workers used in the first days of the project.

Neither dam nor bridge construction could begin until new roads connected the dam site to Highway 89. Twenty-five miles of new road, including a 300-foot blasting job (the Big Cut) through the Echo Cliffs, linked Highway 89 to Page, a town constructed specifically for dam work crews. Convoys of trucks growled over the gear-jamming grade to deliver materials from Flagstaff's railhead, including a prefabricated Glen Canyon Bridge.

Where Highway 89 divides at Bitter Springs, the heavy truck traffic takes the official main highway over the Glen Canyon Bridge, the faster route to Salt Lake City. The old route, now numbered U.S. 89A, leads to the North Rim of the Grand Canyon and the Arizona Strip and rejoins U.S. 89 in Kanab, Utah.

At the Big Cut overlook, the Vermilion Cliffs approach the Echo Cliffs like a pair of pincers, constraining the flow of the Colorado River into deep dark canyons. At one time, a proposal was seriously debated to transform this remote road into an interstate route, extending Interstate 17 from Flagstaff to southern Utah. In the early 1990s, Arizona Governor Fife Symington advocated a super highway route to funnel trade from Mexico to Canada through his home state. Faced with organized political and environmental opponents, the idea went nowhere. Political winds change, free trade agreements with Mexico have faded from the news, but rumors about the extension still occasionally surface.

Some motorists will always press for faster highways. Since its inception, Highway 89 has been straightened, widened and reengineered for safety at ever higher speeds. Abandoned, crumbling bridges, relics of realignment projects, mark the landscape parallel to the highway. Others in less of a hurry will agree with this description from a 1940 Arizona guidebook, and find the landscape "never monotonous; there is always a brilliance of color, constantly changing."

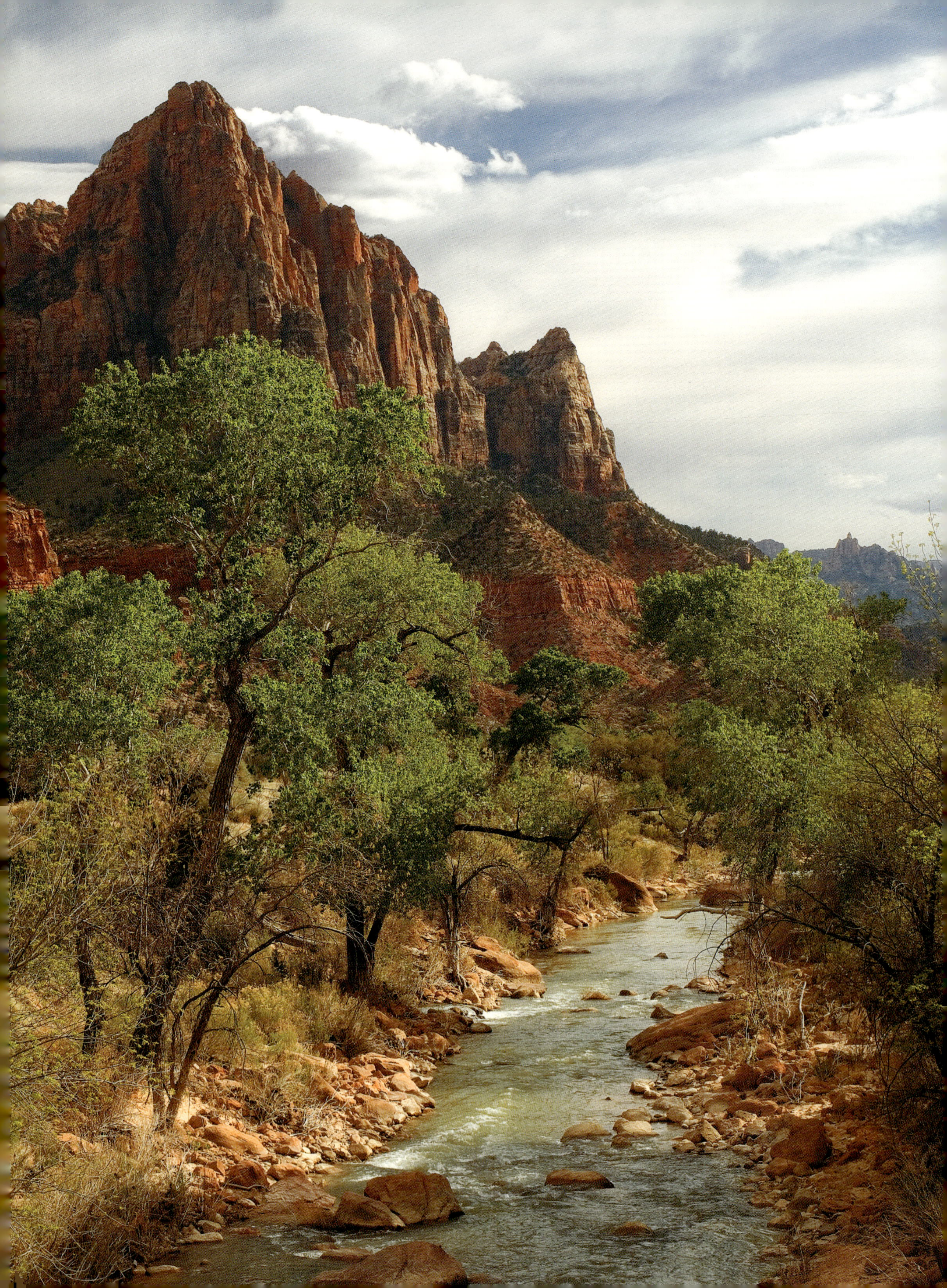

Mormon Heritage Highway
★ ★ ★ Big Water to Thistle, Utah ★ ★ ★ ★ ★ ★ ★

Many Utahns cherish their pioneer heritage, tracing careful genealogies, supporting local history museums and reenacting Mormon emigration trail rides. Pioneer celebrations abound, from the Panguitch Quilt Walk Festival, commemorating the town's heroic survival through its first bitter winter, to Ephraim's pan-Scandinavian cultural weekend. On July 24th, fireworks, parades and rodeos in every town along Highway 89 pay tribute to the date Brigham Young arrived in the Salt Lake valley.

In 2006, a federal bill created the Mormon Pioneer National Heritage Area along Highway 89 from the Arizona/Utah border to Thistle. Declaring that "the landscape, architecture, traditions, beliefs, folk life, products, and events along Highway 89 convey the heritage of the pioneer settlement," the designation encourages the small towns along the corridor to unite in promoting tourism, economic development and heritage conservation. Under the emblem of Highway 89, these communities have joined efforts to retain their rural appeal while adapting to the 21st century.

Gathering of the Saints in Zion

In its first 16 years, the membership of The Church of Jesus Christ of Latter-day Saints (LDS) had been forced out of Ohio, Missouri and Illinois, church founder and prophet Joseph Smith had been murdered while in jail, and "Mormons" had become reviled by the American press for both the practice of polygamy and its intertwined civil and religious administration. In 1846, threatened with more violence in Illinois, LDS Church President Brigham Young led 3,000 followers across Iowa into a winter encampment on the banks of the Missouri River.

Young, whose faith required of him to establish the Kingdom of God in preparation for the return of Christ, sought isolation

WATCHTOWER: U.S. 89 parallels the headwaters of the Virgin River in the Long Valley east of Zion National Park. The river, carving for miles through the Navajo sandstone layer of the Colorado plateau, exits the Zion Narrows into a cottonwood valley enclosed by sheer cliffs soaring upward over 2,000 feet. At the mouth of Zion Canyon, the river bends around the Watchtower (opposite), eventually joining the Colorado drainage at Lake Mead.

PARTY FAVORS: Cowboy hats and barbecue await a French tour group at a Kanab banquet hall. (above)

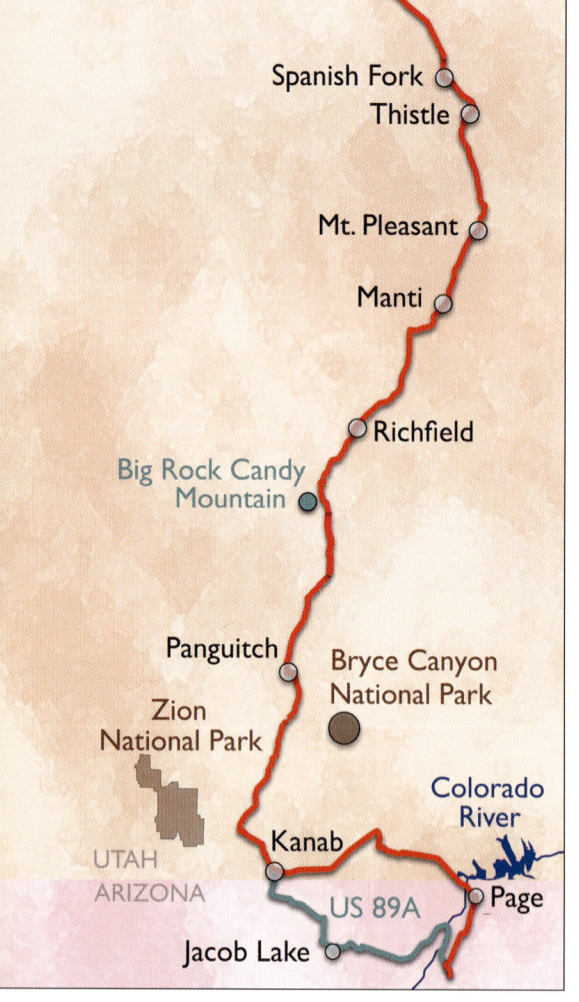

from hostile federal officials and self-appointed vigilante groups. Only a few mountain men, like Jim Bridger, had explored the Intermountain West, territory then claimed by Mexico into present-day Wyoming. Young based his plans on the hope that if the Mormons settled on land considered worthless, they could avoid more conflict. The Great Salt Lake Valley appealed because of its isolation. The Oregon Trail swung to the north while the Old Spanish Trail between Santa Fe and California passed more than 100 miles to the south. The native Utes and Shoshones treated the valley as a no-mans' land between their traditional tribal boundaries. Though rumored to be a barren desert, mountain streams might be channeled to irrigate the sagebrush valley. Survival of the fledgling faith and the Saints depended on whether Mormon farmers could make the "desert bloom like a rose."

MANTI UTAH TEMPLE: In Manti, The Church of Jesus Christ of Latter-day Saints dedicated its third Utah temple (above) in 1888. The Mormon Miracle Pageant is performed at the base of the temple each June.

A SACRED COMMAND: King Mormon and his son Moroni in a pivotal scene in the Mormon Miracle Pageant. (left)

LAMONI'S QUEEN: Cast member in the Mormon Miracle Pageant (opposite)

US HIGHWAY 89: UTAH ★ 67

BIG ROCK CANDY MOUNTAIN: Burl Ives released "Big Rock Candy Mountain" in 1949, a folk song credited to Harry "Haywire Mac" McClintock, a brakeman on the Denver & Rio Grande Railway's Thistle–Marysvale line that passed beneath the mountain. Ives likely had no idea when he recorded the song that it referred to a real place, complete with a "Lemonade Springs."

In the spring of 1847, the Mormons loaded their wagons and headed west, still uncertain about their destination. When Young decided on the Great Salt Lake Valley, he did not reveal it to even his closest advisors. To avoid conflicts, the Mormon pioneers paralleled the existing Oregon Trail on the opposite side of the Platte River. Organized into small companies, the first 1,600 members staged out of Winter Quarters. And even as the first pioneers began to build homes and plant their first crops in Salt Lake in July 1847, thousands more made arrangements to join them in Utah. An overseas proselytizing program chartered entire boats for the emigration of converts, primarily from England, Wales and Scandinavia. The "gathering of Zion" brought an estimated 70,000 members across the 1,300-mile Mormon trail in the years before completion of the first transcontinental railway.

Emigrants clamored at Young for farmsteads and rangeland, and soon waves of wagon trains rolled out from Salt Lake City. After only two years in Utah, the LDS Church assembled families and individuals with the requisite skills for a self-sufficient community and sent them to establish Manti in the Sanpete Valley, followed by more companies into the valleys of the Sevier River and southern Utah. Eventually the "Mormon Corridor" reached from Mesa, Arizona, to Jackson, Wyoming, gaining at least a toe-hold across the Saints' proposed State of Deseret, and establishing the route for much of the future Highway 89.

Even prior to their arrival in Utah, LDS Church authorities had developed a systematic plan for their towns: wide streets lined with irrigation ditches, rectilinear blocks subdivided into fenced home sites, with the church itself at the main intersection. Surrounding farmland was often distributed by lottery. By clustering the houses in villages, the pioneers could protect themselves with fortifications if necessary. Once the basic layout of the town took shape, attention turned to infrastructure projects. Church tithing obligations included a full day of labor in every 10, directed toward construction of meeting houses, forts, schools, bridges and roads.

Brigham Young frequently visited the Utah settlements as church president and the unofficial governor of the State of Deseret, which functioned in parallel to the federally recognized territorial government. The church leadership's annual autumn tour through the southern settlements traced out much of the future route of Highway 89 from Kanab to Thistle.

The provisional State of Deseret elected a surveyor of highways among its first slate of officials in 1848. But much of the road-building fell to local settlers.

Young occasionally issued them specific instructions, telling the Sanpete Valley pioneers to build "a good state road north across the swamp, ditching it well on each side, and building a bridge across the river." By 1864, the *Deseret News* reported that a road had been completed over more than 20 miles of Highway 89's future course between Fairview and Thistle.

Black Hawk War

Brigham Young's policies toward native peoples were shaped by Book of Mormon teachings that American Indians were, in fact, descendants of the lost tribe of Israel, and that the LDS Church was uniquely called to restore the "Lamanites" to their honored status. More pragmatically, Young preached that it was more cost-effective to feed the displaced Utes than to fight them. Since the U.S. Congress declined to resolve native land claims for the first 18 years of the Utah Territory's existence, the encroaching settlers actually held no titles to their lands.

Sanpete Valley Mormons and Utes maintained an uneasy co-existence until April 1865, when a starving group of Utes butchered some cattle from the Manti settlement. A few settlers confronted the Ute party, and in the process insulted Black Hawk, a young man closely related to several powerful Ute chiefs. Black Hawk and his followers retaliated with a series of dramatic stock raids. His successes brought him fame and attracted allies among the neighboring Paiute and Navajo tribes. With the complicity of Anglo and Mexican traders, Black Hawk's men funneled about 2,000 stolen horses and cattle along the Old Spanish Trail to Taos and Santa Fe, New Mexico.

Brigham Young's response to Black Hawk's predations sharply differed from standard frontier practices. Unwilling to ask for protection by U.S. Army troops, who might be redirected to enforce federal anti-polygamy laws, Young ordered the evacuation of nearly all the southern settlements, abandoning newly planted crops in the fields. From Fredonia to Fairview, settlers again loaded their wagons, this time to retreat to the fortified settlements Young had admonished them to build for just such an emergency.

The territorial militia organized patrols and retaliatory attacks, but the more effective strategy of "forting up" prevented Black Hawk from gaining access to the livestock he needed to sustain his alliances. Black Hawk withdrew from the conflict in 1867, although skirmishes continued for several more years until federal troops finally intervened. Resettlement of the abandoned towns along Highway 89, like Kanab, Panguitch, and Salina, began in 1871.

SHARING THE ROAD: Traveling no more than 20 miles per day, this couple had driven their wagon team (below) up Highway 89 from the highlands of Arizona to Mt. Carmel, Utah.

ART IN THE PARKS: Watercolorist Buffalo Kaplinski at work near the Virgin River in Zion National Park. (opposite)

Canals and Communalism

Though still on the northwestern edge of the Colorado Plateau, the headwaters of the Virgin River divide from the northward flow of the Sevier River at the upper slopes of the Long Valley. Pronounced "se-vere" (from a Spanish word for "violent"), the trickling trout stream gains force from the snow melt of the high plateaus. At the headwaters' divide, Highway 89 enters the Great Basin, a watershed extending to eastern California that has no natural outlet to the sea. The Sevier and other northern rivers drain into playas, mineral-accumulating basins, like the Great Salt Lake.

The pioneers needed canals to divert the copious quantities of fresh water flowing past their arid lands. Rather than raise outside capital, like Phoenix's Jack Swilling, Utah's pioneers built their canal system with sweat-equity. Mormon teachings emphasized economic cooperation: the Saints had pooled their resources to make the trek to Utah, and communal work projects were a regular part of settlement life. In 1864, 123 Richfield settlers dug an 11-mile long canal (six to ten feet wide and two feet deep) in less than 40 days. By the end of the century, nine major canals crossed Sevier County, jointly owned by local property holders, who elected a "watermaster" to distribute their shares fairly. Today, in places like

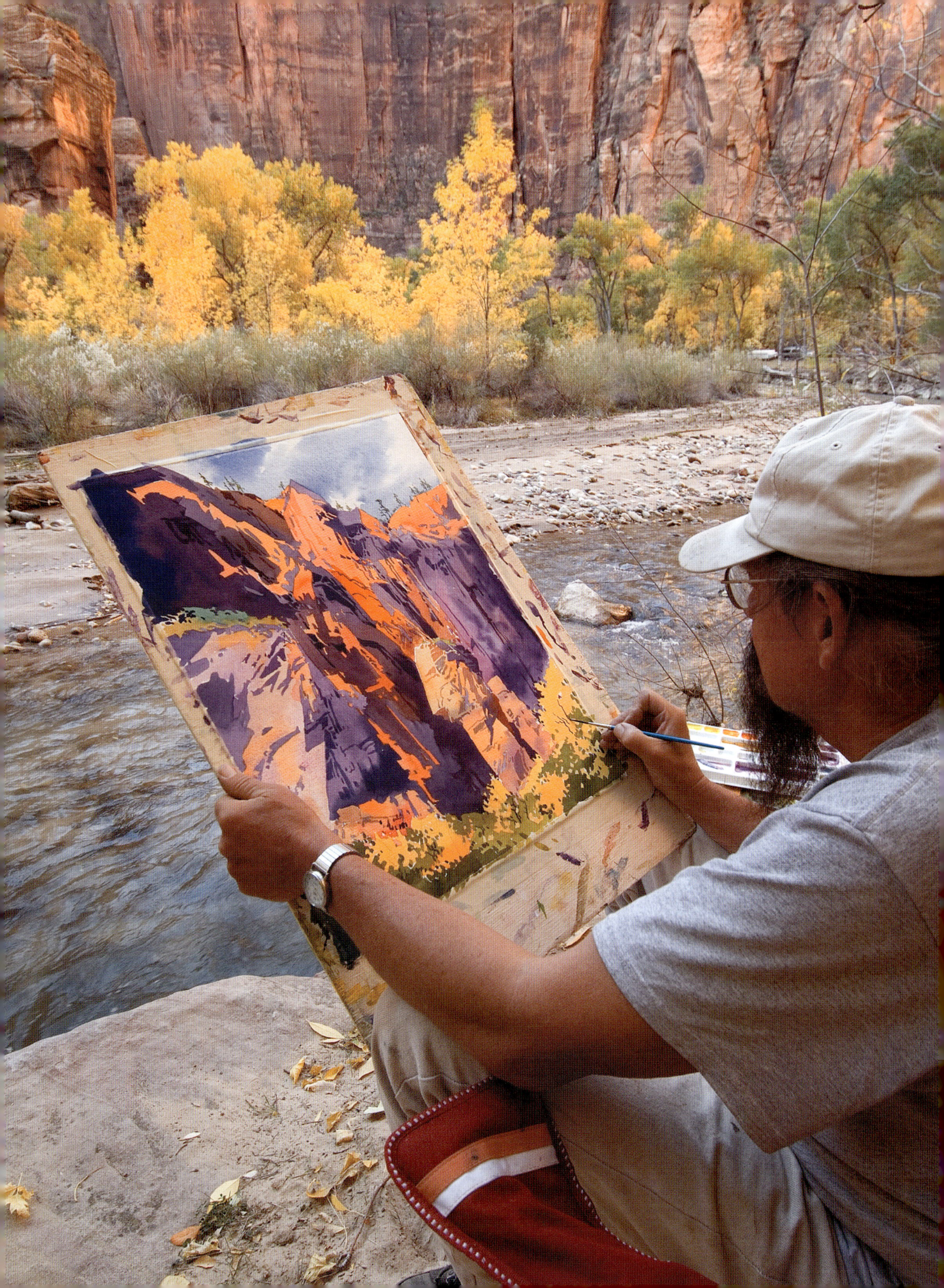

89 Fremont Indian rock art

From about AD 400 to AD 1300, Fremont Indians ranged across Utah's Colorado Plateau and the eastern Great Basin. Prolific creators of rock art, the Fremont left dozens of panels in an area now protected by Fremont Indian State Park, near Joseph. Anthropomorphic figures in the characteristic Fremont-style can be seen from the park's trails, as well as Hunkup's Train. A Paiute Indian, Hunkup drew a panel, alongside the Fremont petroglyphs, to document his trip to the eastern United States in the late 1800s.

Elsinore and Richfield, these canals are still in use, sparkling in the sunshine along Highway 89.

After the Black Hawk crisis abated, Brigham Young spearheaded a period of experimentation in communalism, beginning in 1874, known as the United Order. Participation and enthusiasm for Young's plan varied across the Mormon settlements. In some cases, members deeded some or all of their property to cooperatively-run enterprises. As shareholders, they received proceeds from net income, sometimes drew wages, and always undertook heavy charitable distributions.

Orderville was founded in 1875 when some of the United Order's most fervent practitioners broke away from nearby settlements and instituted some of the period's most stringent practices. At first, leaders of the Orderville cooperative assigned work to every able person (even children), paid men a uniform wage regardless of skill, and served meals in a communal dining hall. While most of the 200 experiments foundered in the first couple of years, Orderville's cooperative was one of the last to dissolve, ultimately undermined by disputes over wages and relaxation of LDS church mandates after Brigham Young's death in 1877.

Unlike the rest of the West, mineral exploration proceeded slowly in southern Utah. Mormon leaders actively discouraged its members from prospecting for heavy minerals. Gold and silver would not feed the poor nor warm winter hearths, and thus could only distract the faithful from their spiritual duties. Nevertheless, gold was discovered in Piute County in 1865, drawing 200 miners west of Marysvale, even as the Mormon settlements remained under evacuation order during the Black Hawk War. Bullion City, the first seat of Piute County, peaked at 1,600 residents. One of a few Utah towns not established by members of the Mormon church, Marysvale became the center of the surrounding mining district. The Denver & Rio Grande Western Railway line branched at Thistle and terminated at Marysvale, making it the first hub for tourists embarking on the Grand Circle of Zion, Bryce and the North Rim of the Grand Canyon.

The Grand Circle
Chocolate, vermilion, white, gray and pink: the cliffs of Utah's Grand Staircase are stacked on a foundation of Kaibab limestone, the same

HOME OF THE HO-MADE PIES: Jack Morrison started his gas station at Mt. Carmel Junction in 1931, as the east entry road to Zion National Park was being completed. His wife served pie to the tourists who traveled the Grand Circle in larger numbers after the opening of the Zion–Mt. Carmel tunnel. Descendants of the Morrisons still run the Thunderbird Restaurant, motel and golf course, and are keeping the sign (opposite) as founder Jack spelled it.

CEDAR BREAKS NATIONAL MONUMENT (above)

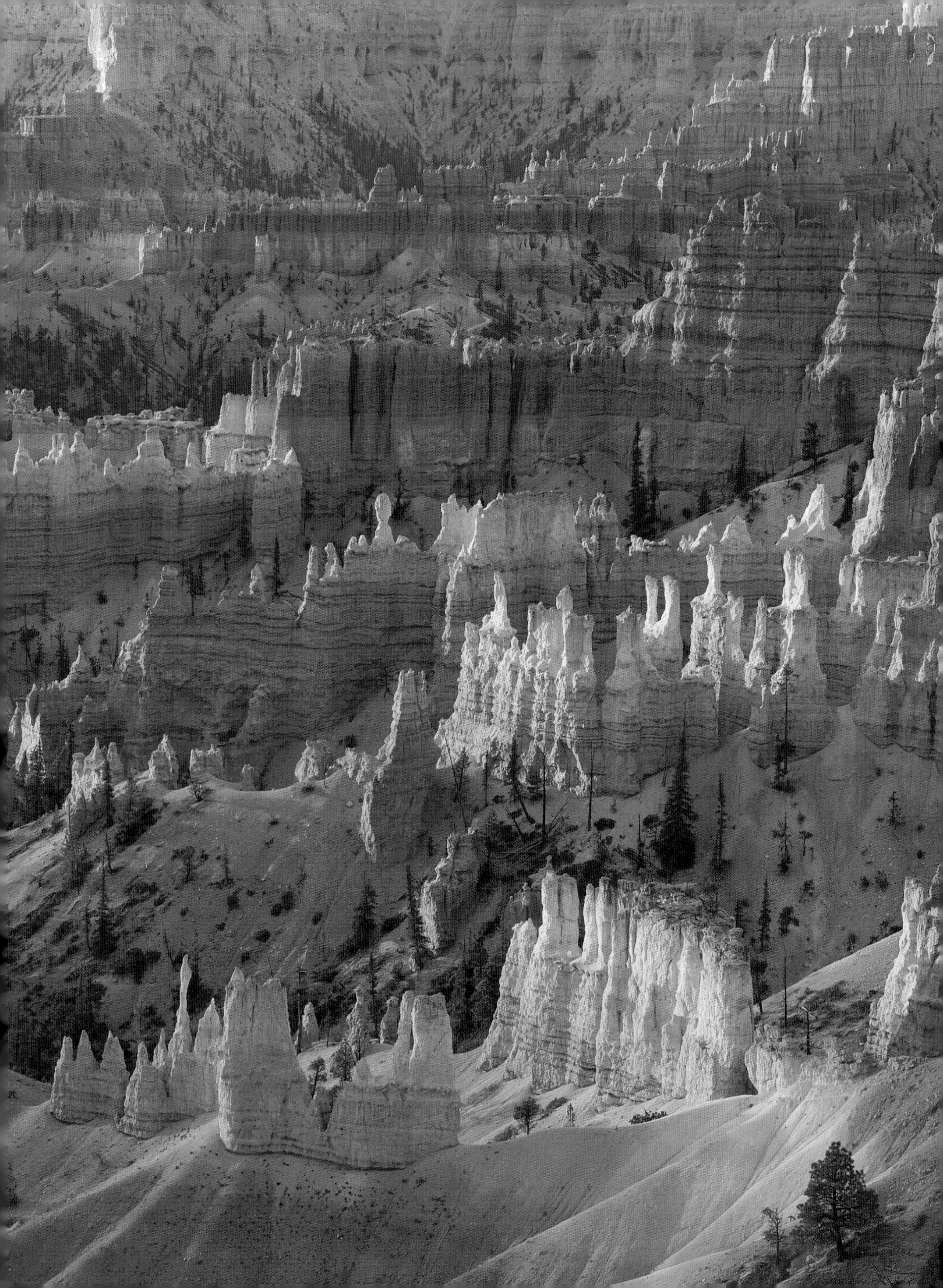

rock formation capping the rims of the Grand Canyon. From Page, Arizona, the modern Highway 89 skirts the southern edge of the Grand Staircase-Escalante National Monument for 60 miles before rejoining U.S. 89A at the base of the Vermilion Cliffs in Kanab, Utah.

Strata of the Grand Staircase blanket southeastern Utah. Erosion exposes individual layers, creating dramatically different landscapes, the provenance of all five national parks in the state. Northward from Kanab, Highway 89 links the two High Plateau region parks, Zion and Bryce. Once atop the Vermilion Cliffs, Zion Canyon's walls glimmer to the west, made of the same Navajo sandstone and Kayenta formations as the White Cliffs. Only 50 miles as the crow flies from Zion's east entrance, Bryce Canyon National Park and Cedar Breaks National Monument are carved from the Claron formation of the Pink Cliffs, the highest and youngest strata of the Colorado Plateau.

Born of sandstone and limestone, shaped by water, ice and wind, all three sites share the same geologic lineage as Grand Canyon National Park, yet it is their unique characteristics that draw millions of visitors. Sunlight plays on the bas relief of petrified sand dunes that formed Zion's 2,000 foot high canyon walls, while shade envelops the verdant corridor of the Virgin River. In Bryce, erosion has nibbled back the plateau into thousands of pinnacles, stair-stepping downward into a giant amphitheatre overlooking the Paria Valley. With a 4,000-foot difference in altitude, the same spring storm frosts

SUNRISE POINT: Bryce Canyon National Park (opposite)

THE SCENIC ROUTE: In the early 1900s, automobile clubs formed to map out motoring trails to scenic locations. Local civic organizations quickly jumped onto the bandwagon to promote "their" highway routes and economies. This sign (above) in Richfield, Utah, is on an old section of U.S. 89 that has been overshadowed by the construction of Interstate 70 to Las Vegas. The wooden sign continues to deteriorate; when revisited in May 2006, it had lost its right-most panel.

Bryce's hoodoos with snow, while rain animates a dozen ephemeral waterfalls tumbling over Zion's canyon walls. Even Bryce Canyon and Cedar Breaks differ, though cut from the same geologic cloth. The Claron formation is more brightly colored at Cedar Breaks, and its rim intimately encircles a smaller amphitheater at the western limit of the Colorado Plateau.

John Wesley Powell visited Zion Canyon in 1872; Brigham Young admired it, but disapproved of giving it the sacred name Mormons reserved for the New Jerusalem. But, unlike the Grand Canyon or Yellowstone areas, no transcontinental trains traversed the red rock country of Utah. When Frederick Dellenbaugh's paintings of Zion were shown at the 1904 St. Louis World's Fair, few Americans even knew the canyon existed.

National Park Service (NPS) Acting Director Horace Albright, on an inspection tour of the western units of the newly created federal agency, first visited Mukuntuweap National Monument in 1917. Albright made it a personal goal to push through the legislation that elevated Zion to a national park (the Paiute name was changed when the park designation took effect in 1919). The majesty of Zion Canyon was so little known that even NPS Director Stephen Mather responded to Albright's enthusiastic report with, "you must have been taken in by the local chamber of commerce." After visiting Zion himself, Mather conceded that Albright was right and became an enthusiastic supporter of the park.

Eager as the local civic community was for tourism business, when Albright visited, even basic facilities were lacking—the nearest accommodations were 100 miles away in Cedar City. When Albright implored Utah Governor Simon Bamberger to improve the highway to Zion, Bamberger angrily shouted (in his heavy German accent), "I build no more roads to rocks!" It took an organized effort of the Arrowhead Trails Association, campaigning for an automobile route from Salt Lake City to Los Angeles (which later became U.S. 91 and then Interstate 15), to spur road improvements to Zion. The distant railway access meant that both Zion and Bryce were developed specifically for the automobile tourist.

Bryce Canyon remained unknown to the general public until 1915, when a ranger persuaded the newly assigned national forest supervisor, J.W. Humphrey, to visit the area. Humphrey immediately sent photographs to Washington, D.C., built a road to the rim the following year, and arranged to publicize the canyon to tourists. News of Bryce Canyon's spectacular scenery reached more potential visitors when *Salt Lake Tribune* columnist Bill Rishel, driving his automobile, "the Pathfinder," published the first driving directions to the canyon for his national audience.

Rather than risk their own vehicles, many early visitors arrived at either the Cedar City or Marysvale rail stations, then were shuttled by local touring companies. In the early 1920s, tourists motored a round-about, back-tracking route around the Grand Circle. The Parry Brothers offered an eight-day tour of the Colorado Plateau, taking in Bryce, the North Rim of the Grand Canyon, Cedar Breaks (a national monument after 1933) and Zion Canyon. Mather and

THREE LAKES CANYON: between Kanab and Mt. Carmel Junction. (opposite, above)

BURRO HEAVEN: Best Friends Animal Sanctuary shelters about 1,700 large and small animals on a 33,000-acre ranch north of Kanab. (opposite, below)

TAXIWAY: Pilot Bob Nalwaker said, "you've got to make your own entertainment out here" before he taxied his ultralight across Highway 89 to the Junction town airport. (below)

CHASING CATTLE: Agriculture has been the mainstay of the economy in Sanpete County since the arrival of the first Mormon settlers. In the early 1900s, farmers raised peas for canneries and sugar beets for industrial processing plants. Most of the row crop farms in Sanpete County have been replaced by cattle, sheep and turkey producers. (above)

HAY TRUCK: Permittees can graze their cattle or sheep on National Forests above the Sanpete Valley during the summer. The animals require supplemental feeding because of cold winters in the valley. (opposite)

Redefining Rural in the 20th Century

As 20th century transportation networks reached rural Utah, the Mormon ideal of agrarian self-sufficiency toppled to new opportunities in commercial markets. Farmers began growing sugar beets for the processing plants opening throughout the state; by 1920, sugar was second to metals in Utah manufacturing. A Gunnison turkey packing plant shipped carloads of dressed birds to New York. Rambouillet sheep bred in Mt. Pleasant founded the bloodlines of herds as far away as Russia and Japan. Currency, scarce in 19th century rural America, flowed from commerce along with the material goods money could buy. Growing automobile ownership created new opportunities: Richfield had a 24-hour repair shop and towing service, the Junction gas station installed a ladies rest room and drinking fountain, and in 1935 the Panguitch newspaper listed the customers patronizing the town's new Ford dealership.

Motoring enlarged small town lifestyles. In the 1920s, nearly every Sanpete County town had a dance pavilion, an explosion of recreational outlets suddenly available five or six nights a week to motoring youth. Automobiles, which symbolized a new standard of living for the American middle class, also powered the exodus of rural Utahns in search of jobs and opportunity during the Great Depression.

Modernization eventually reached Utah's pastoral valleys. In 1937, Sevier County retired its horse-drawn graders for mechanized road maintenance equipment. Hollywood discovered Kanab's red rock scenic locations and movie stars like Maureen O'Hara, Dean Martin and Frank Sinatra filled Kanab's motels for location shooting. Locals often worked as extras: the filming of *Buffalo Bill* in 1943 employed nearly 250 locals and 200 Navajos.

The impact of World War II reached far into southern Utah's agricultural hamlets. Women sewed parachutes at a factory in Manti, soldiers guarded German prisoners of war at a camp in Salina (prisoners were sent from Florence, Arizona, to harvest sugar beets). After Japanese victories cut off supplies of kapok from the island of Java, school children collected milkweed floss to stuff military life vests.

Highways opened up channels to further modernization, but the broad cultural impacts of television were slow to reach southern Utah, as its high mountain ranges blocked signals from Salt Lake City. In 1953, Sevier County had private cable service, but few could afford the $150 installation fee. Heavy voter participation approved bonds

SCANDINAVIAN FESTIVAL: Ephraim celebrates its Scandinavian heritage in an annual cultural festival. The region is known as "Little Denmark" due to the large number of Danish Mormon converts who settled in the valley in the 1850s. (right)

THISTLE: Decades after the 1983 flood devastated the community of Thistle, its ruins still stand in water beside Highway 89. (above)

WINTER PASTURE: The Eliasons of Fountain Green are some of the last sheep ranchers in Sanpete Valley to move their herds from summer grazing lands to winter pasture on foot on Highway 89. (opposite)

to build a 1958 translator for Sevier County; the Lions Club raised funds to bring the public airwaves to Kanab in 1965.

The Thistle Landslide

The northern end of the Mormon Heritage Highway, where Highway 89 joins U.S. 6, is the site of one of Utah's most costly natural disasters. In 1983, a landslide destroyed the town of Thistle, then home to about 50 people. At the confluence of the Spanish Fork River and Thistle Creek, the riverbed, highway and the Denver & Rio Grande Railway tracks crowded into a steep valley. Rio Grande personnel first noticed that the rails had shifted out of alignment in a frequently unstable area downstream from Thistle. Runoff from a wet winter had supersaturated the slopes and within hours, a slow-moving landslide created a natural dam. U.S. 6/89 buckled, then was submerged; the Rio Grande salvaged its tracks. In less than two weeks, the Rio Grande began drilling tunnels to re-route their lines. Rains continued and water rose as much as six feet per day. Contractors raced to place diversion conduits to prevent the lake from overtopping the landslide, weakening the dam and unleashing a potentially deadly flood. Private boat owners formed the "Thistle Navy" to lasso and tow floating buildings away from the outlet. Working nonstop shifts, the Rio Grande reopened the line in less than three months, while U.S. 6/89 remained closed until winter. Highway 89's roadbed was re-routed to higher ground and the Rio Grande trunk line to Marysvale was abandoned. A few submerged buildings are all that remain of Thistle today.

In southern Utah, the post-war interstate highway program overlaid Highway 89 only for a few miles, becoming Interstate 70 between Salina and Elsinore. The interstate shortened the Denver to Los Angeles route, but U.S. 89 remains the north-south backbone of the region. In 2006, the five Utah counties served by the Mormon Heritage Highway had fewer residents than the city of Flagstaff. Development is beginning to impact the areas closest to the Wasatch Front; a $100 million resort is under construction in Kane County. Though treasuring its rural roots, the rest of the region is changing as well: cowboys wear cellphone holsters on their belts and the Kanab public library offers wireless Internet. What remains is the kind of community spirit, reminiscent of the pioneers' cooperative efforts, to stage the local rodeo, county fair or Pioneer Day parade and sustain their small towns. Though few in number, the people living along Highway 89 work to keep their heritage alive, not as a tourist attraction, but as a priceless treasure to pass on to their children and grandchildren.

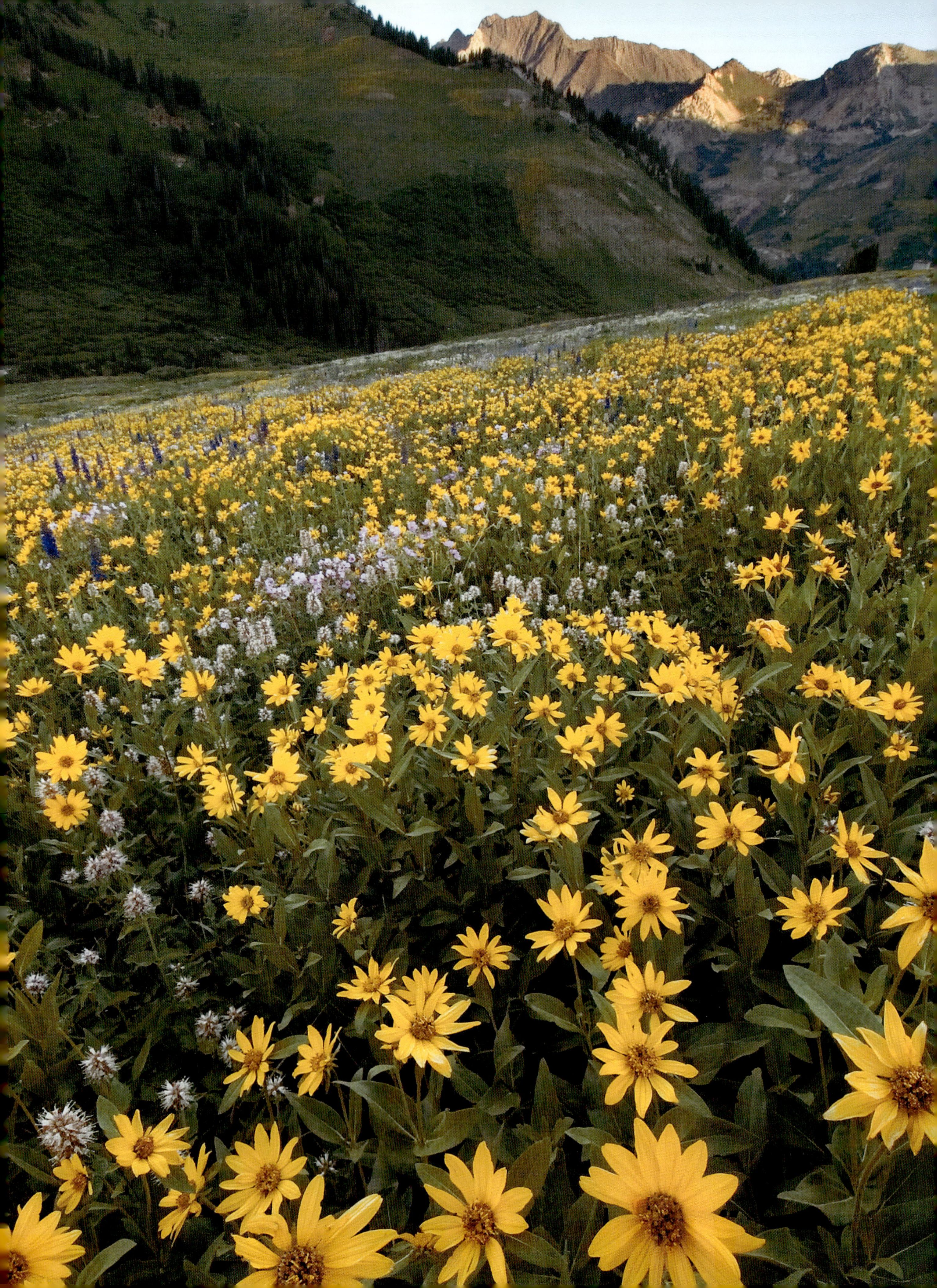

The Wasatch Front
★ ★ ★ Spanish Fork to Garden City, Utah ★ ★ ★ ★ ★ ★

Not even their 1847 flight into the desert valleys beside the Great Salt Lake could completely isolate the fledgling society of The Church of Jesus Christ of Latter-day Saints (LDS). California-bound forty-niners stopped for a rest and never left. Federal soldiers and lapsed converts stayed. Jewish and "gentile" merchants brought goods to Utah markets. The outside world offered new technologies: LDS Church President Brigham Young welcomed innovations like electricity and the telegraph. When it was clear that the Union Pacific and Central Pacific railway lines would meet in Utah to form America's first transcontinental railway, Young negotiated to make Ogden its junction point. Major branch lines serving Los Angeles, Las Vegas, eastern Idaho and the copper mines of Montana met in Ogden and Salt Lake, creating the commercial hub of the Intermountain West.

The railways were a conduit for the first large numbers of non-Mormons descending into Utah for economic opportunity rather than faith. Italians, Greeks, Slavs and Mexicans established churches, institutions and traditions in various corners of Salt Lake City and Ogden. Mines, factories and market farmers offered wages and opportunity for thousands arriving at the turn of the century, just as the LDS society was adapting from a self-sufficient agrarian ideal to the rising material expectations of a rapidly industrializing America.

In the 1920s, the nation's growing network of automobile trails, from Chicago and Denver to California and Oregon coastal cities, converged on Salt Lake City. By 1925 more than 1,500 motor vehicles per day traversed the state highway over the "Point of the Mountain" between Salt Lake City and Lehi. Bill Rishel, automobile editor for *The Salt Lake Tribune* and one-man Utah tourism promoter, distributed vast quantities of pamphlets and advice to transcontinental motorists heading to Salt Lake City, emblazoned with the slogan "Center of Scenic America."

ALBION BASIN: The Wasatch Mountains average 300 inches of snowfall per year. At high elevations, like Albion Basin in Little Cottonwood Canyon, snow may remain until mid-June. At the end of July, dozens of species of wildflowers attract thousands of human aficionados, nourish migrating hummingbirds, and support a small moose population. (opposite)

CAPITOL MOTEL: Neon from competing motels (above) once greeted travelers on State Street leading into downtown Salt Lake City.

US HIGHWAY 89: UTAH ★ 85

Rishel's maps invariably included State Street, festooned with highway and trail markers for the 14 named routes that converged in Salt Lake City before the federal highways were numbered. Highway 89 represents one strand of a braided story that intertwines America's legendary mountain men, war heros and diverse immigrants into a 21st century Utah.

Water in the Desert: Lake Bonneville and the Great Salt Lake
From Spanish Fork to Brigham City, Highway 89 straddles the dividing line between the Great Basin and the westernmost peaks of the Rocky Mountains. The Wasatch Front rises 7,000 feet above the level valley floor, a basin once covered in sagebrush and wildflowers. The heavily forested mountains receive as much as 300 inches of snowfall. The steep terrain makes for Olympic-class ski resorts, but impossible

86 ★ THE WASATCH FRONT

ENGINE 844: The Union Pacific Railway maintains the historic steam engine #844, (opposite) which regularly stops at the Ogden Union Station on tours of the Western states.

STATE STREET: State Street, particularly the section from Brigham Young's Eagle Gate to the Salt Lake City/County Building, has hosted a plethora of events, from a parade to promote the city's 1943 World War II bond drive, the public celebration when Salt Lake City was awarded the 2002 Winter Olympic Games, to the honoring of the University of Utah football team's undefeated 2008 season.

WELLSVILLE MOUNTAINS: The Wellsville Mountains of the Wasatch Front (above) rise steeply between the Great Salt Lake and the Cache Valley of northern Utah. A raptor flyway was discovered along its ridges; volunteers monitor autumn hawk migrations from its peaks. The original formula for Dr. Pierce's elixir contained both alcohol and opium, no doubt contributing to his success. From Buffalo, New York, Dr. R.V. Pierce's mail-order business sold nearly a million bottles of patent medicine each year.

FORT BUENAVENTURA: In 1825-26, fur trappers over-wintered in the Ogden area in a large encampment. Fur trading companies outfitted the trappers, advanced supplies and traps, organized them into parties and sent them out for a season. The "Mountain Men" collected beaver pelts in the fall and spring, caching their furs to exchange for supplies at a summer rendezvous. Each summer, modern day re-enactors (opposite) organize encampments throughout the mountain man territory.

conditions for building water storage dams and much of the spring runoff flows directly into the Great Salt Lake. With 85 percent of the state's population living in a 100-mile band along the front, Utahns increasingly depend on reclamation projects from the central and eastern parts of the state to bring water to their communities.

The empty glacial cirques crowning the Wasatch Mountains recount a much wetter climate, as do the tiered shorelines etched along the base of the mountains. The Great Salt Lake and its fresh water feeder, Utah Lake, are vestiges of Lake Bonneville, which covered northwestern Utah and parts of Nevada and Idaho. Lake Bonneville's former shorelines are 870 feet higher than the Great Salt Lake's surface level. About 14,500 years ago, Lake Bonneville suddenly overtopped its threshold near the Utah–Idaho border. Hydrologists estimate that as its floodwaters emptied into the Snake River, the nearly 20,000-square-mile lake dropped 350 feet in less than a year. The intermediate level, which geologists call Lake Provo, lasted long enough to build intermediate shorelines, which are now favored building sites along the Wasatch Front. As the climate became drier, the lake dropped below its outlet and mineral-laden runoff began to concentrate in the contemporary Great Salt Lake.

The Great Salt Lake

Rising in a spring tide fed by snowmelt and evaporating as much as two feet in Utah's hot summers, the Great Salt Lake covers an area some 75 miles long and 35 miles wide. Runoff from four major tributaries produces a cline from freshwater bays to maximum salinity at the lake's center. Longer cyclical wet and dry periods have sometimes reduced the lake's level by as much as 20 feet from its average height, the shoreline in some places retreating 15 miles.

The Great Salt Lake shoreline is mostly mud flat, reeds or upland grasses, with few sandy beaches. While some fishes can tolerate the brackish margins, only two animal species live in the main body of the lake: brine flies and brine shrimp. Brine shrimp eggs by the ton are commercially harvested each year for fish farm food. Also using the abundant food resource are migratory shorebirds: as many as five million birds use the Great Salt Lake as a staging point during their migration. Some 500,000 Wilson's phalaropes spend August feeding on brine shrimp and flies to fuel the last legs of their flight from the Arctic tundra to wintering grounds off the coast of Baja California. Birdwatchers comb the shoreline to spot Great Basin specialties like Clark's grebes and white pelicans.

Several bathing resorts once catered to locals and tourists who wanted to swim in the buoyant water of Great Salt Lake. On the south end of the lake, the LDS Church built Saltair, the "Coney

[89] Fried Chicken to go

Harlan Sanders licensed his secret recipe for chicken fried in a pressure cooker to Pete Harman, a Utah restaurant owner. In 1952, Harman opened the world's first Kentucky Fried Chicken franchise, on Highway 89 at the corner of State Street and 3900 South in South Salt Lake. Harman invented the now iconic paper bucket, and helped to introduce the take-out food concept to America's highways.

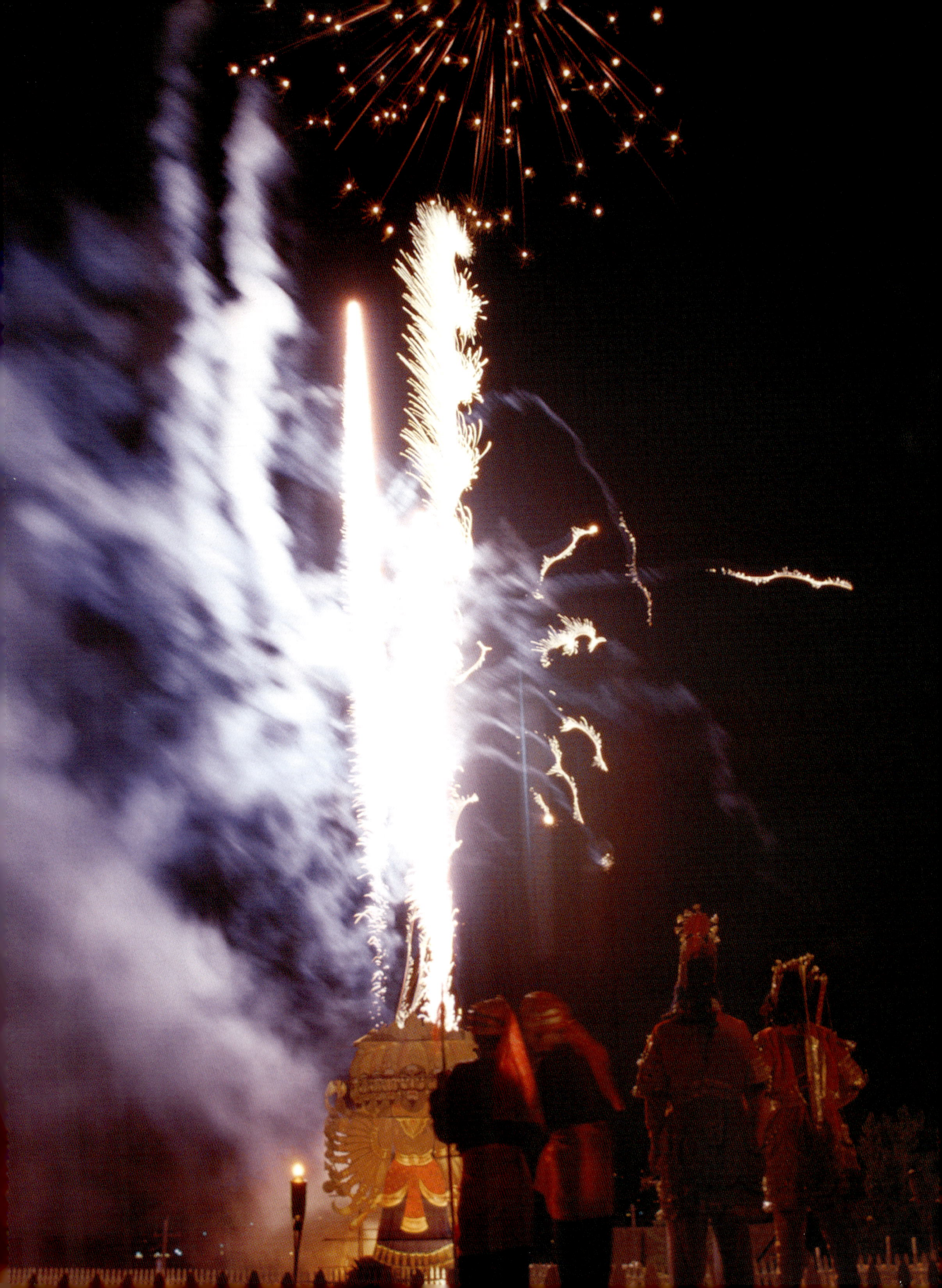

Island of the West," in 1893 to provide a "wholesome" recreation destination for its members. By the 1920s, the Saltair resort drew nearly 500,000 patrons a year with entertainment like a roller coaster, merry-go-round and dancing to live music.

Simon Bamberger, the future governor, built a privately held electric tramway that connected Salt Lake City to Ogden. In 1896, Bamberger moved structures from another lakeside resort to a create a new destination directly on his tram line. Lagoon featured a spring-fed lake for swimming and boating, dance pavilion, fun house and horse racing. Despite his interest in the tramway, Bamberger hosted the state's first "good roads" meetings at the resort in 1908. As late as 1927, Lagoon could advertise itself as Utah's only resort on a paved road. Over the decades, Lagoon has become a local landmark and Highway 89 overlooks its roller coasters and water-park rides.

The State Street River

In the early days of the Utah Territory, State Street began at the main entrance to Brigham Young's private holdings, adjacent to Temple Square. Later extended to the foot of the Utah State Capitol and widened (while preserving the famous Eagle Gate to Young's estate), State Street drew a ruler-straight line southward for miles before arcing over the Point of the Mountain into Utah County.

The record precipitation in the winter of 1982–83 and the same late spring conditions that resulted in the Thistle landslide stalled the

FIREWORKS FINALE: Devotees of the Hare Krishna movement bought an A.M. radio station in Spanish Fork in 1982, expanding on the site to operate a llama farm and ultimately build the Sri Sri Radha Krishna Temple, helped by a $25,000 donation from The Church of Jesus Christ of Latter-day Saints and volunteer labor from local Mormons. The temple hosts several popular festivals throughout the year. At India Fest, the Pageant of the Ramayana concludes when the hero's flaming arrows (opposite) destroy the 10-headed mythological villain-king.

OLYMPIC PARK: After the 2002 Winter Olympic Games, the University of Utah campus reinstalled the Olympic cauldron outside the venue for the opening festivities, along with the Hoberman Arch (above) used during the medal award ceremonies. The torch was relit to mark the opening of the 2006 Olympic Games in Turin, Italy.

US Highway 89: Utah ★ 91

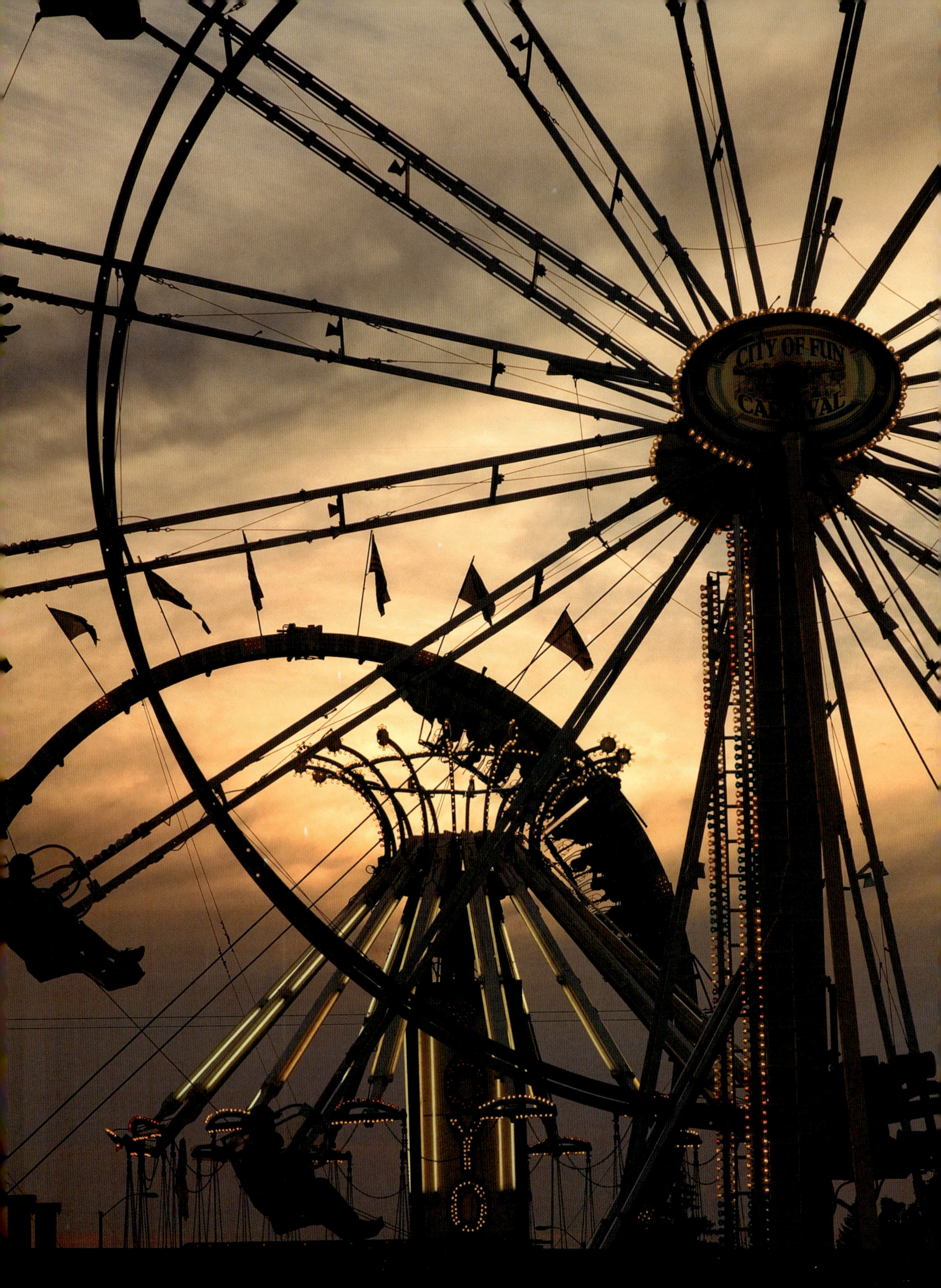
CITY OF FUN
CARNIVAL

snowmelt in the Wasatch Mountains. A sudden transition to 90 degree temperatures brought water gushing down City Creek Canyon into downtown Salt Lake City. While businesses and Temple Square were sandbagged, city officials watched as the stream continued to rise over Memorial Day weekend. On Sunday morning, the city and church leaders' emergency calls mobilized an estimated 8,000 volunteers to sandbag a mile-and-a-half long temporary channel down State Street. Within hours, the creek was safely diverted into the canal. Mayor Ted Wilson later described the effort as "the biggest street festival ever." As the waters raged for two weeks, the city extended the canal southward several more blocks. Two rapidly-constructed four-lane bridges linked downtown to Interstate 15; temporary pedestrian bridges provided a popular lunchtime stroll for downtown office workers and tourists who came to see the "State Street River."

Mountains and Mountain Men

Northern Utah's first American explorers were fur traders who traveled extensively through its mountains but left few traces: historians continue to debate the exact locations of the fur-trading encampments in Cache Valley. The first fur-trading operations sent men to trap along the Missouri River tributaries, a natural conduit to the St. Louis, Missouri, markets. By the time William Ashley and his partner formed the Rocky Mountain Fur Company in 1822, access

PEACH DAYS: South of Brigham City, Highway 89 is known as "Fruit Way." Since 1904, the surrounding area has celebrated the harvest during Peach Days. Family fruit stands still line the highway, local peaches abound in dutch-oven cobblers, and now 75,000 people attend the parade (above), concerts and carnival (opposite) each September.

US Highway 89: Utah ★ 93

PROM NIGHT: Maddox Ranch House fronts Highway 89, and has been serving prom night couples since 1949. (above)

FESTIVAL OF WIND: David Hoggan of Berkeley Kite Wranglers improvises to loft kites at the Festival of Wind in Spanish Fork. (opposite)

to the best sites on the Missouri River was tightly controlled by their competition. Working south, Ashley's team found virgin trapping lands in southwestern Wyoming and northern Utah. However, exploiting the fur-rich region required a new scheme to bring the pelts profitably to the East. At first, individual trappers traveled for months each year to St. Louis to trade for the next season's supplies. Instead, Ashley and his field leader, Jedediah Smith, instituted the summer rendezvous in 1825. By resupplying the men at an annual summer gathering, Ashley kept the men in the field year-round, where they could trap beaver in the fall and spring when their pelts were the thickest and most valuable.

Trapping ceased during winter when streams and rivers froze. Beginning in 1824, Ashley's men gathered in encampments to rest, repair traps and socialize, overwintering the first year in Cache Valley. In that first camp, the men speculated and wagered on the course of the Bear River to the west of the valley. To settle the dispute, a young Jim Bridger built a rawhide boat and floated through the Bear River Canyon to the Great Salt Lake. Traditionally, Bridger is credited with being the first American to visit the lake, although historians now suggest another trapper, Etienne Provost (for whom the town of Provo is named), actually reached its shores earlier that fall. Heavy snows drove the trappers to the Great Salt Lake near Ogden the next year, but they returned to Cache Valley for the following two winters.

In the summer of 1826, Ashley chose Cache Valley (named for caves trappers dug to store their furs) for the second rendezvous. The "stupendous mountains," trapper Daniel Potts wrote in an 1826 letter to his brother, "are unrivaled for beauty and serenity of scenery." At the end of the rendezvous, Ashley sold out to Smith, but remained Smith's agent, returning to St. Louis with $60,000 in pelts.

Jedediah Smith held the 1827 and 1828 rendezvous on the southern end of Bear Lake. With trade goods and alcohol available, the gatherings grew into raucous affairs, drawing independent trappers and local Indian tribes, as well as Ashley's men, for days and weeks of trading and socializing.

The heyday of trapping in northern Utah lasted only four or five years before shifting northward. Prices peaked in 1834; by 1840, as fashionable Eastern men discarded beaver hats in favor of silk, profits plummeted. Jim Bridger set up a trading post in Wyoming, where he met Brigham Young at the head of the 1847 Mormon exodus and advised him on passable routes to the Salt Lake Valley. Intimately familiar with the region, mountain men like Thomas "Broken Hand" Fitzpatrick turned to guiding emigrant wagon trains on the Oregon Trail, using much of the route pioneered for the Ashley rendezvous caravans.

89 Peaches for a President

Franklin D. Roosevelet stopped in Brigham City, Ogden and Salt Lake City during his 1932 campaign for president. Roosevelt spoke for 45 minutes at the Salt Lake Tabernacle. In Brigham City, the reigning Peach Days Queen presented him with five cases of peaches.

BEAR RIVER MIGRATORY BIRD REFUGE: One in four of the world's American avocets (above) visits the Great Salt Lake ecosystem (top) during migration each year.

SHRIMP BOATS: Brine shrimp boats docked at the Antelope Island Marina at the start of the autumn harvest season. (opposite)

STATE STREET: Named State Street in the Salt Lake Valley, U.S. 89 leads to Utah's Capitol. (following pages)

96 ★ THE WASATCH FRONT

Few Oregon Trail wagon train emigrants detoured southward to Cache Valley. With the beaver trapped out, and with its harsh winters, Cache Valley was mostly ignored for the first years of Mormon settlement in Utah. Crowded grazing conditions on the western side of the Wasatch Mountains led pioneers to forage cattle in the valley in 1855, although an especially severe winter proved fatal for much of the herd. Undaunted, a church-sponsored mission established the first permanent settlement at Wellsville the following year.

Logan became a regional center, both because of the 1884 completion of the LDS Church's second temple and the 1888 founding of the state agricultural college (now Utah State University). Today, about 100,000 people live in Cache Valley, and Highway 89 climbs over those "stupendous mountains" to link the Logan metropolitan area to the Wasatch Front.

Agrarian to Metropolitan

With many spokes of the nation's transportation systems converging in the Ogden/Salt Lake corridor and with access to material inputs like coal and iron, Utah had integrated into the industrialized economy by the dawn of the 20th century. Copper mines supplied raw materials for wire to meet the nation's demand for electricity. A steel mill opened in Provo. Train yards shipped carloads of Utah's sugar, along with its cattle, sheep and wool.

Once firmly enmeshed in the national economy, the Wasatch Front suffered along with the rest of the country in the Great Depression. A third of Utah's workforce was unemployed in 1932. Two hundred people encamped near the railway viaduct at the mouth of Weber Canyon in Utah's largest "hobo jungle." The Egyptian Theatre in Ogden raffled off Chevrolet automobiles to bring in business, packing the ballroom with thousands for the drawings.

The woes of the Great Depression outweighed traditional Western and uniquely Mormon resistance to growth of the federal government. The Civilian Conservation Corps (CCC) funded long-needed revegetation of the mountainsides, after generations of sheep-herding had left areas like Farmington vulnerable to disastrous mudslides in 1923 and 1930. The CCC also built the Springville Art Gallery to house the high school's $150,000 collection of art (acquired by the students and funded by electing the annual art queen at a penny per vote). Largely due to 30,000 public works jobs, Utah's unemployment fell to 6 percent in 1936.

Geography propelled northern Utah into the forefront of World War II. Military planners recognized the convergence of railroads and highways at Ogden and its pivotal location relative to ports on the west coast. The city was a logical site for an explosives stockpile when military planners relocated much of its ordinance away from the Eastern seaboard after World War I. As the military eyed the growing strength of imperial Japan, Ogden won a major air base beyond "sea-based air bombardment." Hill Field, built mostly with federal Works Progress Administration funding, employed about 600 civilians when Japan bombed Pearl Harbor. By 1943, their ranks had

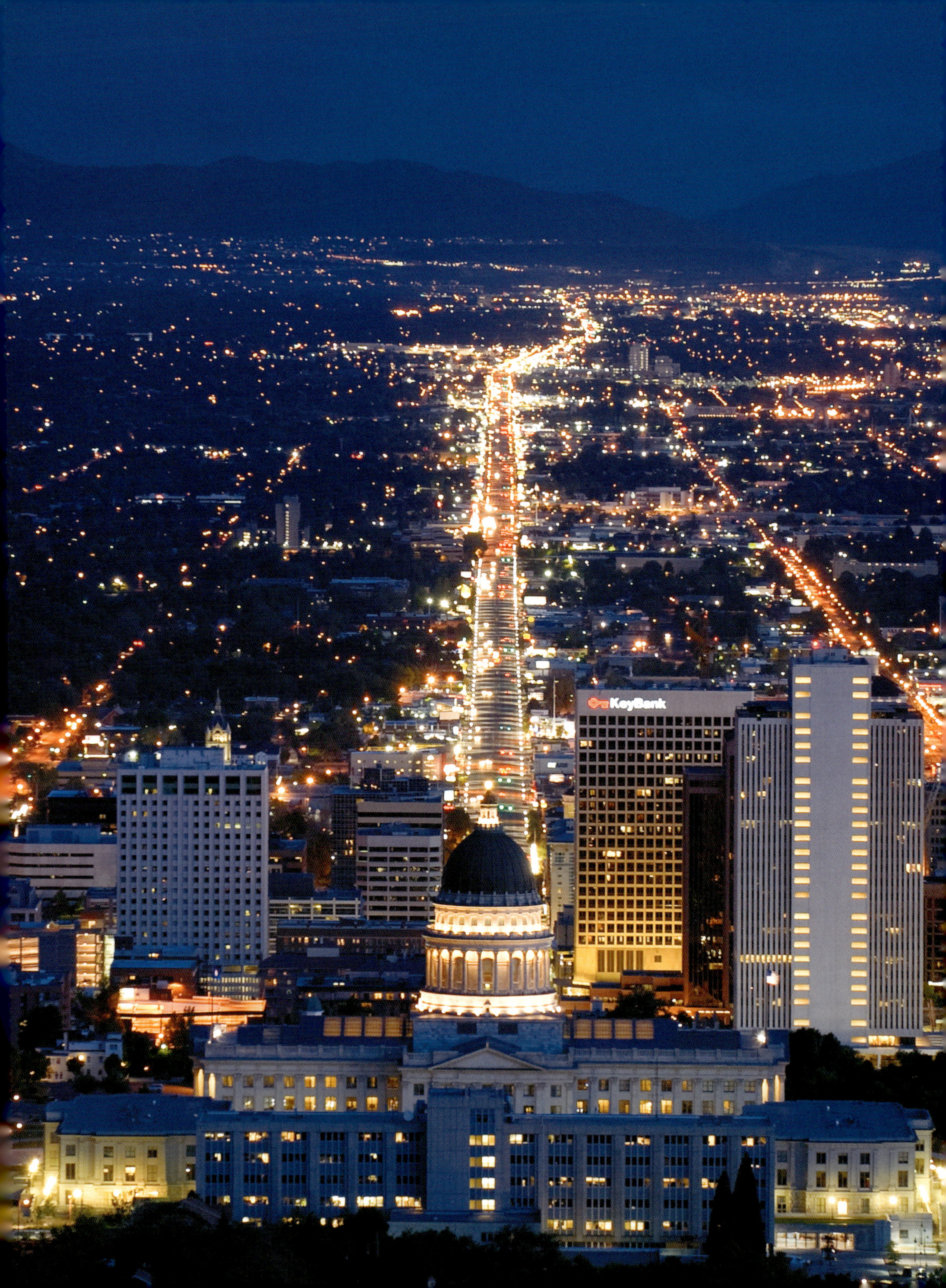
KeyBank

swelled to 15,700 workers repairing and maintaining the military's aircraft fleet.

The Japanese naval threat led the U.S. Army Ninth Service Command to relocate its headquarters to Fort Douglas, next to the University of Utah campus in Salt Lake City. As the command post for operations west of the Rockies, thousands of recruits passed through the fort, temporarily housed in trailers at the school's football stadium until new buildings were completed.

Utah's workforce could not meet the sudden demand for labor. More than 70,000 of the states' native sons and daughters joined the armed forces even as the war factories demanded an influx of new workers. After tapping women, the elderly (including at least one 99-year-old) and high schoolers, plants recruited out of the state. Clearfield Naval Station brought in Navajo and Pueblo Indians, as well as 2,400 African Americans from the Southern states.

Only about 680 African-Americans lived in Utah in 1900, many of them attached to an all-black army company at Fort Douglas in Salt Lake City. Small communities came together in Salt Lake and Ogden, where black-owned businesses catered exclusively to black porters working for the Union Pacific and Southern Pacific railroads. The Railway Porters and Waiters Club contracted with both lines to house their black employees during Ogden layovers. Prior to World War II, Utah's societal attitudes mirrored those of much of America: a color-line, formal or informal, barred African-Americans' access to hotels, restaurants, theatre seats, even home ownership in entire neighborhoods.

African-American soldiers training at Ogden before shipping out to the Japanese theatre effectively desegregated Ogden's notorious saloon district. The soldiers, heading into overseas combat, were in no mood to tolerate refusals of service by 25th Street barmen. According to one local, rather than acquiesce, the soldiers would simply "tear up the place." Ultimately, barroom owners decided that it was more profitable to serve the soldiers.

Japanese immigrants came to Utah in large numbers in the 1880s, when anti-Chinese emigration laws restricted that source of labor in the West. Settling along the Wasatch Front, many purchased their own farms, and Japanese farmers became well-known for their quality celery and strawberry crops. The Japanese community fostered its heritage through the Ogden Buddhist Temple (founded in 1913), Japanese language newspapers and language schools for their children.

At the beginning of U.S. involvement in World War II, President Franklin Roosevelt signed an emergency decree, requiring first generation Japanese immigrants and their American-born children to relocate away from the West Coast. The Utah population of Japanese swelled, both from voluntary evacuees and those sent to the Topaz internment camp in the far western desert. Along the Wasatch Front, citizen committees passed resolutions and pressured real estate agents to prevent evacuees from buying Utah farmland; at the same time many farmers relied on internment labor to harvest their crops. When the camps closed after the war, many Japanese remained in Utah to restart their shattered lives.

Greeks formed one of the largest immigrant communities in Utah, numbering more than 20,000 by 1915. Labor agents recruited young men either in Greece or at the landing docks, promising jobs in exchange for wage kickbacks. Picture brides followed, and a new generation grew up studying their parents' language in after-school sessions and attending Eastern Orthodox services at Salt Lake City's Holy Trinity Church. The church's Mother's Organization bazaar begun in 1935 has grown into one of Utah's largest cultural celebrations. Today, the Greek Festival attracts upwards of 50,000 people for four days of food and cultural activities in the heart of the old "Greek Town."

More waves of immigration continued to reshape northern Utah after the war. LDS Church missionary efforts in the Pacific Islands resulted in sizable Tongan and Samoan communities in Salt Lake City by the 1960s. Vietnamese refugees settled in the Salt Lake Valley after 1975. Long-standing Latino communities expanded, first with the arrival of Central Americans fleeing political turmoil in El Salvador, Nicaragua and Guatemala, then from other states as construction boomed in preparation for the 2002

ASSEMBLY HALL: Constellations of holiday lights illuminate the plaza surrounding the Salt Lake City-based headquarters and Temple of The Church of Jesus Christ of Latter-day Saints. The temple grounds mark the origin for the Cartesian grid used as street addresses for Salt Lake City and its surrounding communities. The Assembly Hall was the second building constructed in the complex and now hosts free music concerts in the holiday season.

CULTURAL COLLAGE: (clockwise from top left) Ukrainian-style egg decorating at Salt Lake City's Living Traditions Festival; Utah Pride Festival-goers in front of the Salt Lake City/County Building; Bridal menhdi at the Hindu community's Sri Ganesa Temple; float in Salt Lake City Pioneer Day parade; Serbian blacksmithing demonstration at the Living Traditions Festival.

Winter Olympic Games. At 11.2 percent in 2006, Latinos now form Utah's largest minority community.

Opportunities at Utah's three research universities have attracted faculty and students from around the world; some graduates stayed to launch companies or pursue their own academic careers. Utah's growth in software, medical devices and other technology industries have joined tourism as major elements of the state's contribution to the global economy.

From Highways to Freeways

Back in 1920, highway improvements had led one newspaper editor to eagerly predict that one day, "Davis County would a continuous city from Salt Lake to Ogden." By the late 1950s, new housing developments north of Salt Lake City had spawned an urgent traffic problem. New federal highway programs under President Dwight Eisenhower provided funding for a ready solution. Governor George D. Clyde launched Utah's interstate building program in January 1958 by ceremonially bulldozing a dairy barn to break ground for a six-mile stretch of freeway, Utah' first segment of Interstate 15.

While the first federal routes, like Highway 89, had become major arterial routes in urban areas, the design of controlled access freeways

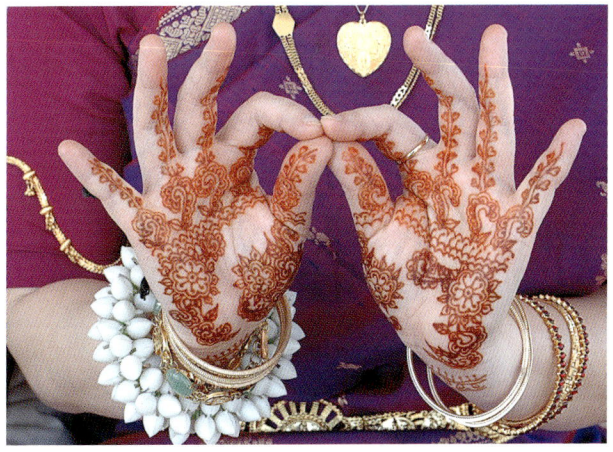

US Highway 89: Utah ★ 101

BEAR RIVER MIGRATORY BIRD REFUGE: Even in the frigid winter, the Bear River Migratory Bird Refuge (above) teams with life. About 70,000 tundra swans migrate from the Arctic region to overwinter on Utah's southerly ice and feed in open water. While the Great Salt Lake itself does not freeze due to its high salinity, the refuge encompasses the freshwater outlet of the Bear River and its surrounding flood plains. Up to 5 million migrant waterfowl, waders and passerines use the margins of the Great Salt Lake during their annual migratory cycles.

LOGAN CANYON: Seven state or National Forest scenic byways have been created on segments of Highway 89, including Logan Canyon Scenic Byway. (opposite)

compromised business access for efficiency and speed. Local opposition to diverting traffic from village centers, and rising costs of land in suburban areas complicated the interstate construction program. Lehi's city council organized a petition drive to protest the I-15 route through their town, complaining that it would take away valuable acreage from housing development and future tax rolls. State and federal road officials promised five underpasses and two cloverleaf exchanges; Lehi dropped its objections.

Along the Wasatch Front, I-15 replaced U.S. 91 while leaving large segments of U.S. 89 intact. Much of Highway 89, particularly the eastern bench sections in Utah, Weber and Box Elder counties, serves as an important business route for local communities, while State Street remains a primary arterial route for Salt Lake County.

The metropolitan Wasatch Front looks vastly different from that which Brigham Young toured in his carriage, or from Bill Rishel's published motoring routes in 1911 for roads little better than wagon tracks. More than a century-and-a-half later, automobile trails have overlaid the pioneers' ruts, followed by highways and interstates: roads for a state whose population now is interwoven from many cultural layers, merging into a multicultural future that will again redefine the West.

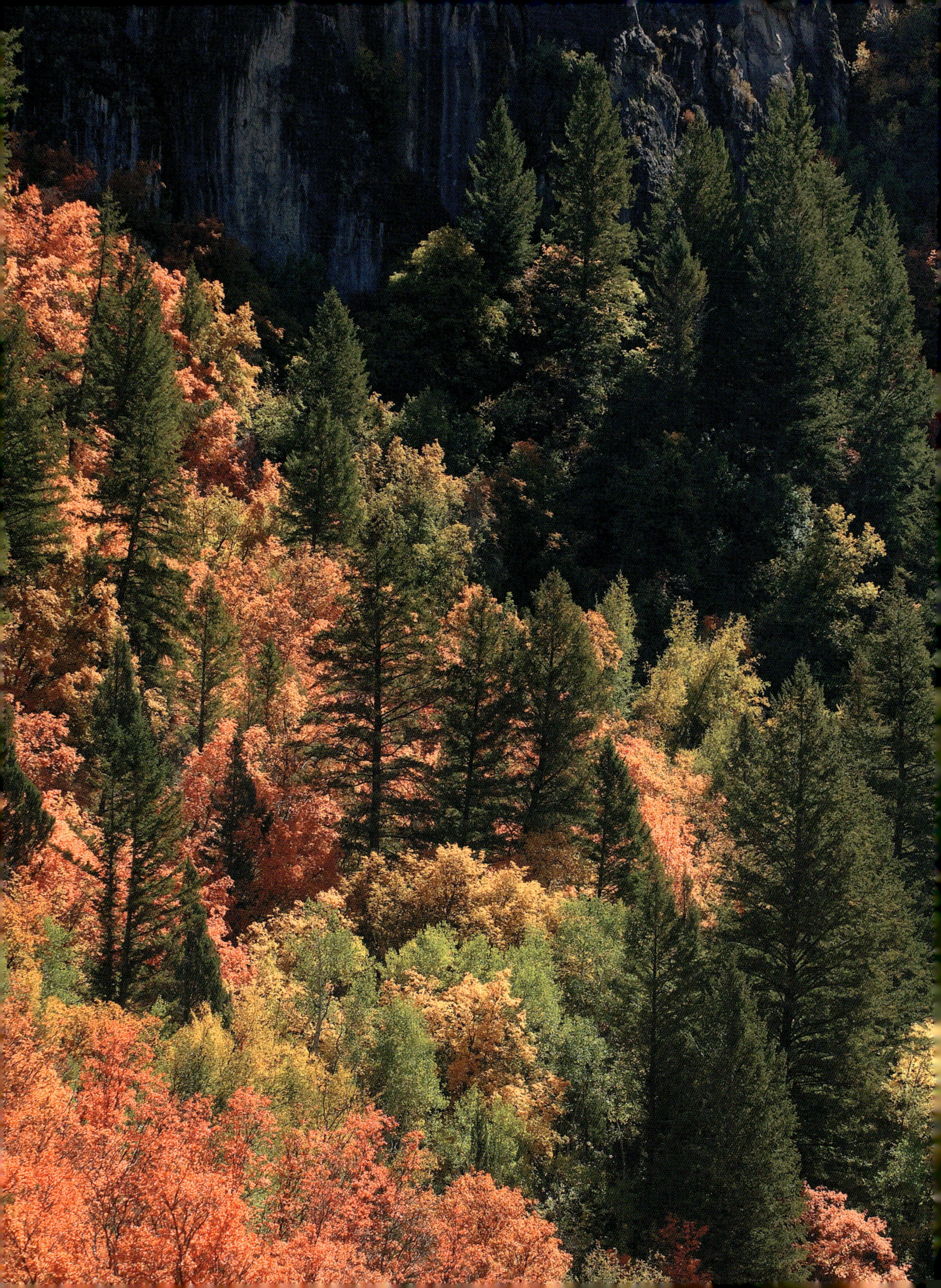

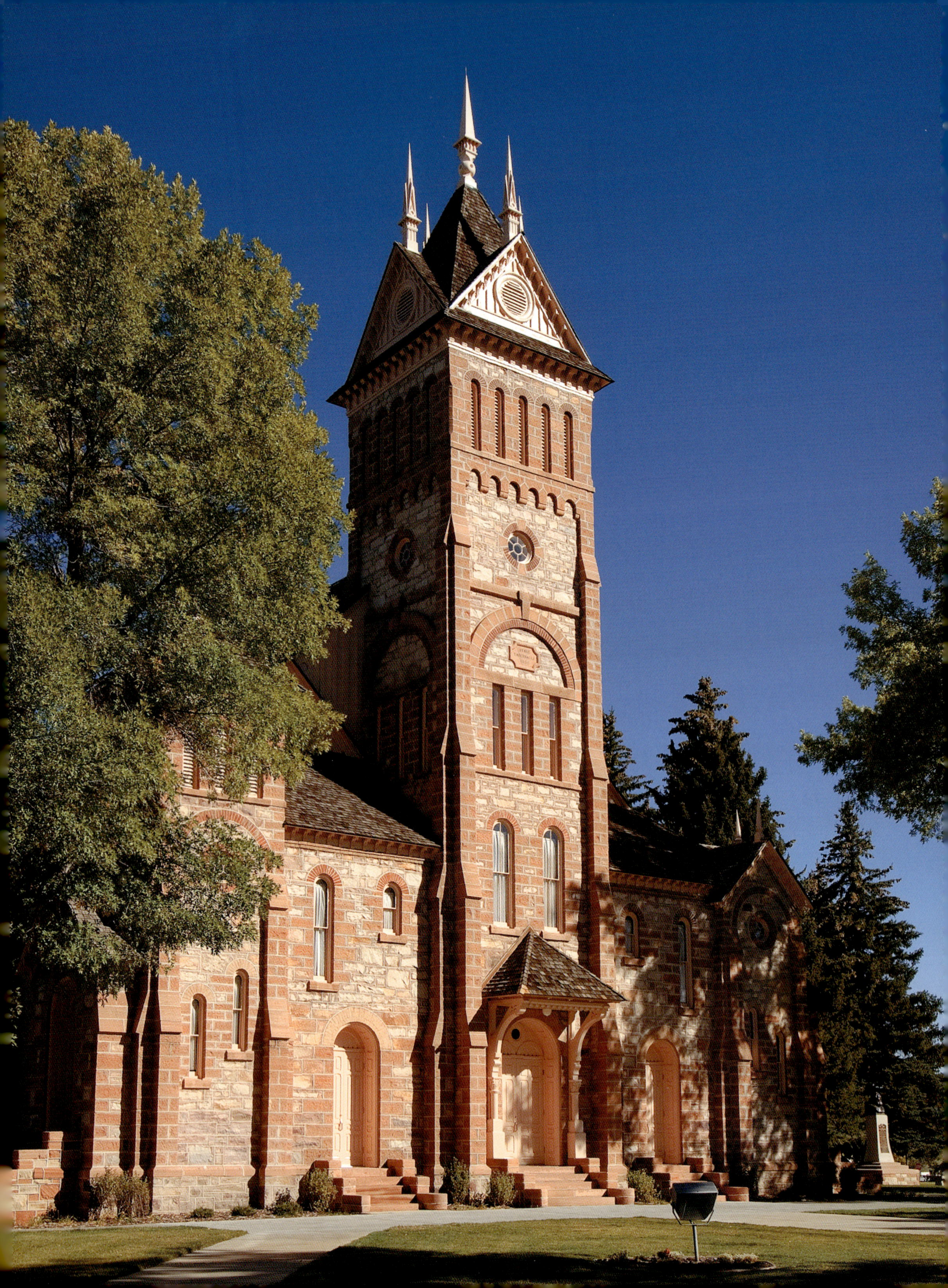

Riding with the Committee
★ ★ ★ Fish Haven to Geneva, Idaho ★ ★ ★ ★ ★ ★ ★

The National Scenic Byway program recognizes routes because of their "intrinsic qualities" in any of six categories: archaeological, cultural, historical, natural, recreational or scenic value. The designation process begins with a proposal from a self-organized community group to the state byway coordinator. Once approved at the state level, byway committees can apply for federal grants and further recognition by the Federal Highway Administration as a National Scenic Byway. Seven state or national forest byways have been established on segments of Highway 89. In Idaho, two dozen local tourism boards, government agencies and businesses supported the successful 2001 Oregon Trail–Bear Lake Scenic Byway proposal. The byway includes U.S. 89 from the Utah–Idaho border to Montpelier, Idaho, where it turns westward to parallel the Oregon Trail on U.S. 30.

Touring with the Byway Committee
Early in the 2007 tourist season, the newly reconstituted Oregon Trail–Bear Lake Scenic Byway Committee undertook a survey of its domain. In earlier incarnations, the committee had produced a successful byway proposal and carried out the initial work of marking the route and installing interpretive panels at several waypoints. On this bright June Saturday, a new crop of volunteers, mostly from civic organizations in towns along the route, climbs onto a rented shuttle bus to learn first-hand about the byway program.

At its first stop, the committee celebrates an achievement: the installation of an interpretive sign, which committee chairman Tony Varilone has bird-dogged for four years. The concept came from an earlier planning session and, with help from the National Park Service, the panel was designed and produced for $700 in 18 months. Negotiations with various highway jurisdictions required two-and-a-half more years to complete the project. State traffic

PARIS TABERNACLE: The Paris Tabernacle cost $50,000 to build in 1884–89. In 2004, The Church of Jesus Chris of Latter-day Saints launched a $1 million dollar renovation of the structure. (opposite)

ALL-AMERICAN ENTRYWAY: Highway 89 widens to four lanes, but slows to 25 miles per hour as it passes through the main street of Paris, Idaho. (above)

engineers selected a hillside location above the roadway, necessitating a wheelchair ramp to the sign and a steel staircase to stop erosion where visitors had climbed the bank instead of using the ramp. Varilone entertains the committee by reciting a bountiful list of acronyms and agencies involved in erecting the single panel.

Points of Interest

The next order of business is to locate the missing monument to Idaho native son Gutzon Borglum, the sculptor of Mt. Rushmore. The polygamous Borglum family actually produced two famous sculptors, but only Gutzon was born in St. Charles, Idaho. (His brother and rival, Solon, was well known for his Western bronzes, like the *Rough Rider* sculpture in the town square of Prescott, Arizona). A large stone tablet engraved with the pertinent facts had recently been removed from the roadside; the committee needs to know whether to budget for a replacement.

106 ★ Riding with the Committee

The bus pulls behind the St. Charles city hall/fire station. The greeting committee, the mayor and a city councilman, quickly point out the Borglum monument leaning against the wall next to the fire engine. The town had rescued it from toppling over in unstable soil and secured it until they decided where to reinstall it. A brainstorming session erupts: a fine location next to the city hall is available–can the highway be widened to park recreational vehicles? What about a parking lot, picnic tables, an actual Borglum sculpture? The mayor's concerned expression relaxes at the mention of government grants, long-range planning and an invitation to add a town representative to the committee. The mayor declines to join the group as they climb onto the bus.

From the shuttle bus window, the landscape definitely meets the "scenic" criteria. Shafts of sunshine flash between timbers of old wooden barns. Mares nurse wobbly foals. Green hay fields roll down to the shoreline. The mineral composition of the water gives Bear Lake an unusual azure blue hue. The contrast to the blue sky is striking this summer morning, but the old-timers insist that the color is most beautiful in the late afternoon.

No one on the committee proposes an interpretive sign about the Bear Lake Monster, said to be 100 feet long, as fast as a galloping

COMMITTEE AT WORK: The Oregon Trail–Bear Lake Scenic Byway Committee receives a private tour of the Paris Tabernacle. (opposite)

AMERICAN WHITE PELICANS: Bear Lake National Wildlife Refuge (above)

US Highway 89: Idaho ★ 107

horse, frightfully spewing water from its many mouths. Joseph C. Rich, son of the valley's pioneer leader, first reported the terror in a letter to a Salt Lake City newspaper in 1868. Although cynics suggested that Rich invented a legend to publicize the Bear Lake region and his spa, monster sightings frightened witnesses for decades.

Paris: Gateway to Yellowstone

The traffic slows to 25 mph as the bus enters Paris, population 600. The 1863 Bear Lake valley pioneers, having miscalculated the location of the Idaho border, elected representatives to the Utah territorial legislature until a 1872 Idaho survey corrected the error and enrolled them in that territory's tax base. That's how Paris became the seat for Bear Lake County and the Paris Tabernacle became The Church of Jesus Christ of Latter-day Saints' (LDS) first organized center outside of Utah.

Hosts Roger and Janene Pugmire show the byway committee around the newly renovated tabernacle. Completed in 1889 by local volunteers laboring alongside Swiss masons, it serves as the LDS Church's spiritual and administrative center for the surrounding 50-mile area. The red sandstone was hauled 18 miles from the opposite side of Bear Lake, by wagon in summer, by sled over the frozen lake in winter. A former shipbuilder installed the nautical-style ceiling. The renovators took care to preserve the extensive "grained" millwork, a laborious hand-finishing treatment that makes the locally harvested pine resemble oak and other hardwoods. Janene points out her favorite round window.

LDS leadership positions are unpaid, filled by members called to service, often for years at a time and far from home. The Pugmires are native to the Bear Lake valley, and the tabernacle is a treasure in their personal and family histories. Janene shares with the committee visitor statistics from the tabernacle guest book. Roger recalls when Highway 89 was called the Yellowstone Highway, the route to the park from Los Angeles via Salt Lake City.

Heading northward again, the highway jogs through the village of Ovid. The most prominent structure is a vacant LDS ward house now in private hands. The graceful lines and faded wood siding suggest a potential opportunity for a bed and breakfast; someone on the bus pipes up, "the owners won't sell."

Montpelier has a historical marker describing how Butch Cassidy's gang robbed the local bank in 1886. The town does not commemorate another famous theft, carried out by members of Coxey's Army. Times were tough in 1894, and hundreds of unemployed protestors

LDS MEETINGHOUSE: Ovid (opposite, above)

DINNER FOR TWO: National Oregon/California Trail Center serves visitors from around the world by day, and as a community resource by night, hosting theatrical productions in its auditorium and exhibitions and private parties in its reception area. (opposite, below)

LOCAL FAUNA: Farm implements find a new life in a field north of Montpelier. (above)

BEAR LAKE: Limestone minerals give Bear Lake its unusual azure color. (following pages)

were riding the rails to a demonstration in Washington, D.C. Union Pacific Railroad management became nervous about appearing to support the protest and sidetracked the boxcars in Montpelier. Some of the stranded men broke into the roundhouse, started up two of the engines and headed east. Running the red signals on the track, they were arrested in Cokeville, Wyoming, only 30 miles away.

Commemorating the Oregon Trail

The centerpiece of the Oregon Trail–Bear Lake Scenic Byway (and the intersection of Highway 89 and U.S. 30) was an important waypoint on one of America's great westward migrations. Over 300,000 emigrants used the Oregon Trail, which was really a network of wagon routes from Independence, Missouri, to Oregon City, Oregon. Some pioneers made the journey independently, while others relied on former mountain men to lead their wagon trains safely across the more than 2,000 miles of dangerous terrain.

Emigrants considered the "Big Hill," east of modern-day Montpelier, to be one of the most treacherous segments of the Oregon Trail. The ascent was challenging, but bringing the wagons down the summit in a controlled descent demanded skill and brute force. Wagon masters locked or tied down their wheels to slow their momentum, and at times, lowered the wagons with ropes wrapped around trees.

After enduring Wyoming's high desert, crossing the Continental Divide and summiting the Big Hill, the Clover Creek area was a welcome respite for the emigrant trains. Camps along the Bear River, with its abundant fresh water and shady wooded banks, afforded a relatively comfortable place to rest while livestock grazed on lush native grasses, and to regroup for the next major leg of the trail across Idaho's western deserts in the lower Snake River basin.

The first emigrant wagon train reached Oregon in 1843, and for two decades thousands more followed, until the first transcontinental rail link was completed in 1867. A few hardy pioneers continued to travel the overland route by wagon through the 1880s. By then, Clover Creek had long been settled by Mormon homesteaders, although when Brigham Young sent his followers to Clover Creek, he also renamed the town Montpelier, after the capitol of his home state, Vermont.

A stone pillar, overshadowed by a covered wagon replica, marks the Clover Creek encampment at the crossroads of U.S. 89 and the Oregon Trail. Ezra Meeker emigrated to the Oregon Territory in 1852. In 1906, he reversed his journey, traveling by covered wagon to place these markers along the trail before the ruts faded entirely from the land. The 76-year-old Meeker drove his wagon across the Brooklyn Bridge and to the White House (President Theodore Roosevelt came out to see his oxen) to campaign for the trail's preservation. Meeker continued into his 90s to travel the Oregon Trail by wagon, automobile and airplane, publicizing the trail and advocating for a transcontinental highway along the route.

Out of the 2,170-mile Oregon Trail, only about 300 miles of wagon ruts are still visible, mostly on private property and none accessible from the scenic byway. No one is more aware of this fact than Becky Smith, the director of Montpelier's National Oregon/California Trail Center. Her visitors jolt along in a simulated covered wagon, learn how the pioneers fitted out their expeditions for the months-long journey, and explore a re-created Clover Creek emigrant camp. Becky tells the committee that her visitors' most frequent question is where they can see the "real trail." The intersection of U.S. 89 and U.S. 30, marked by Meeker's pillar, is Clover Creek camp's historic location, but a paved highway is not what the visitors have in mind. Varilone makes another note for the committee's report.

Long afternoon shadows play across the last miles of the byway tour. The committee will draft large and small goals into their new master plan. Varilone envisions about 100 visitors a day spread along the byway interpretive sites. Organized tour companies plan their schedules three years in advance, so Smith sees a victory in every new bus arriving at the Oregon/California Trail Center. Highway 89 may never see a Borglum statue, a new public beach on Bear Lake or even a walking path along the Oregon Trail. But, it just might happen: it takes only one or two leaders in a rural community to get exceedingly difficult things done.

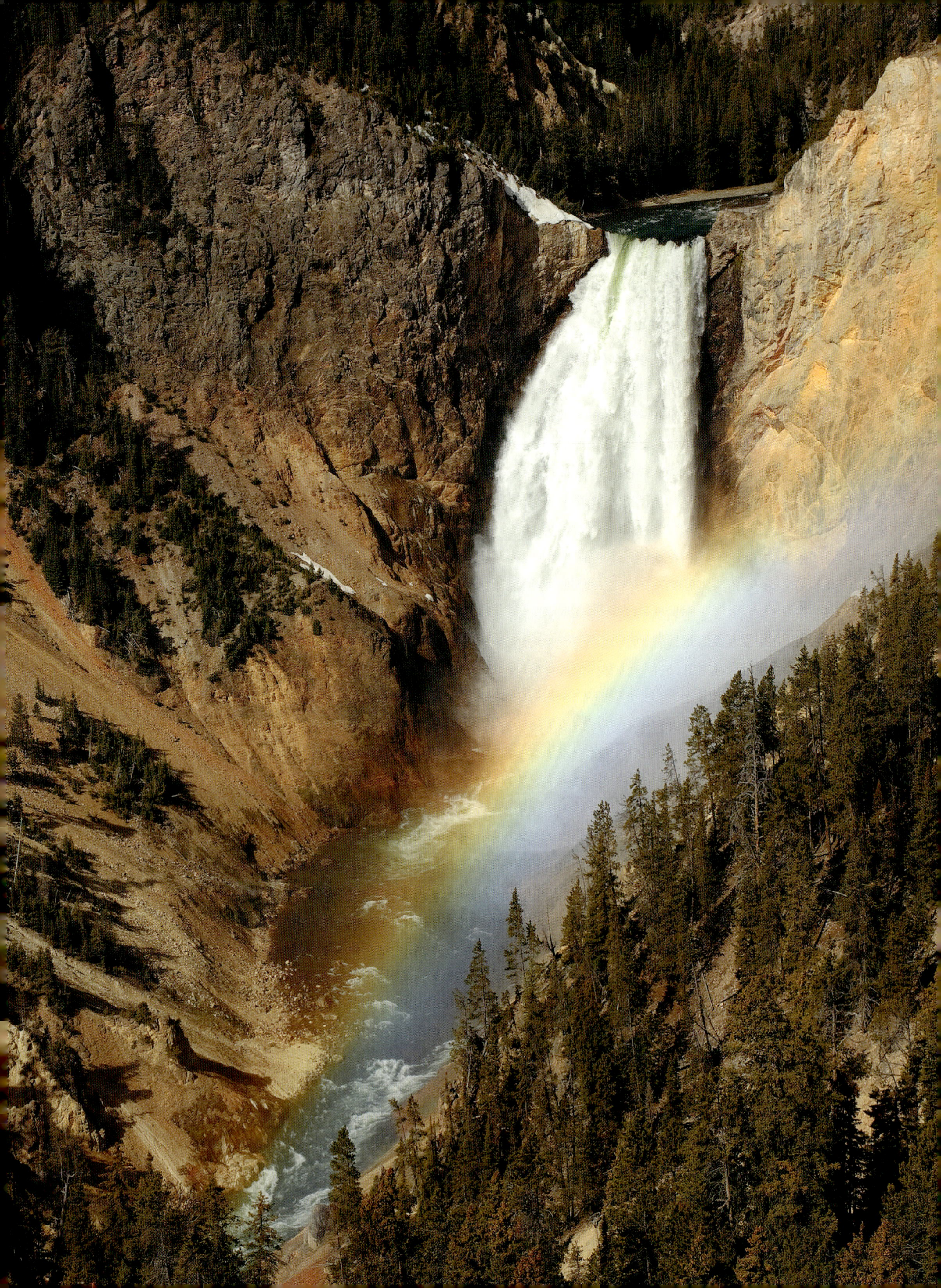

Greater Yellowstone
★ ★ ★ Star Valley, Wyoming, to Yellowstone National Park ★ ★ ★

Before the 1926 primary highway system was mapped, politicians had quibbled for more than a decade over how (and whether) to give the federal government a role in interstate road construction. In the vacuum of indecision, coalitions of private citizens and municipalities built the nation's first transcontinental automobile routes. From 1912 to 1930, the Yellowstone Trail Association promoted a "Good Road from Plymouth Rock to Puget Sound." Civic leaders organized trail-building days and pot-hole filling campaigns. Volunteers painted trail markers, a black arrow on a yellow background, on rocks, barns and telephone poles from coast to coast. In their campaigns, the trail organization used the lure of Yellowstone National Park to attract transcontinental motorists away from alternate routes like the Lincoln Highway and the National Old Trails Road.

Adventurous travelers could drive to Yellowstone National Park, but upon arriving at the gates, the first motorists found them firmly shut to automobiles. The park's stagecoach concessionaires, intent on preserving a near monopoly in transporting railway-arriving tourists, argued (with some factual basis) that Yellowstone's roads could not accommodate both horse-drawn vehicles and automobiles. Enthusiastic motorists brought congressional pressure onto the Department of the Interior for access to the park's roads (automobiles were already permitted in Mount Rainier and Glacier national parks). National Park Service Director Stephen Mather ordered a road-sharing scheme to separate stagecoach traffic from motor vehicles and opened Yellowstone to automobiles on August 1, 1915. Nearly 1,000 motorists drove the park's Grand Loop in the final weeks of the 1915 tourist season.

Informally, many roads to the park's entrances were known locally as a "Yellowstone Highway," including the "Salt Lake–Yellowstone Route" in Bill Rishel's 1927 *Salt Lake Tribune* Automobile Tour Book. Rishel's directions presage almost the entirety of the future Highway

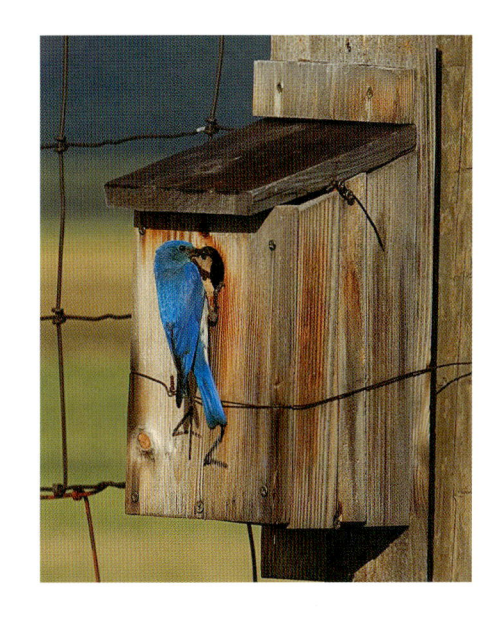

LOWER YELLOWSTONE FALLS: Yellowstone National Park (opposite)

MOUNTAIN BLUEBIRD: Volunteers installed nesting boxes (above) on the boundaries of the National Elk Refuge and other sites around Jackson. An ongoing citizen science effort maintains the boxes and reports nesting successes.

ICE COLUMN: To keep irrigation pipes from freezing and bursting, Star Valley farmers leave them trickling throughout the winter, building up massive columns (right) over the course of the season.

AFTON'S ANTLER ARCH: Afton used over 3,000 antlers to create its landmark elk antler arch (opposite, top) in 1958. It weighs over 15 tons and spans 75 feet across the entire Highway 89.

RURAL FARM DELIVERY: Spring in Star Valley (opposite, bottom)

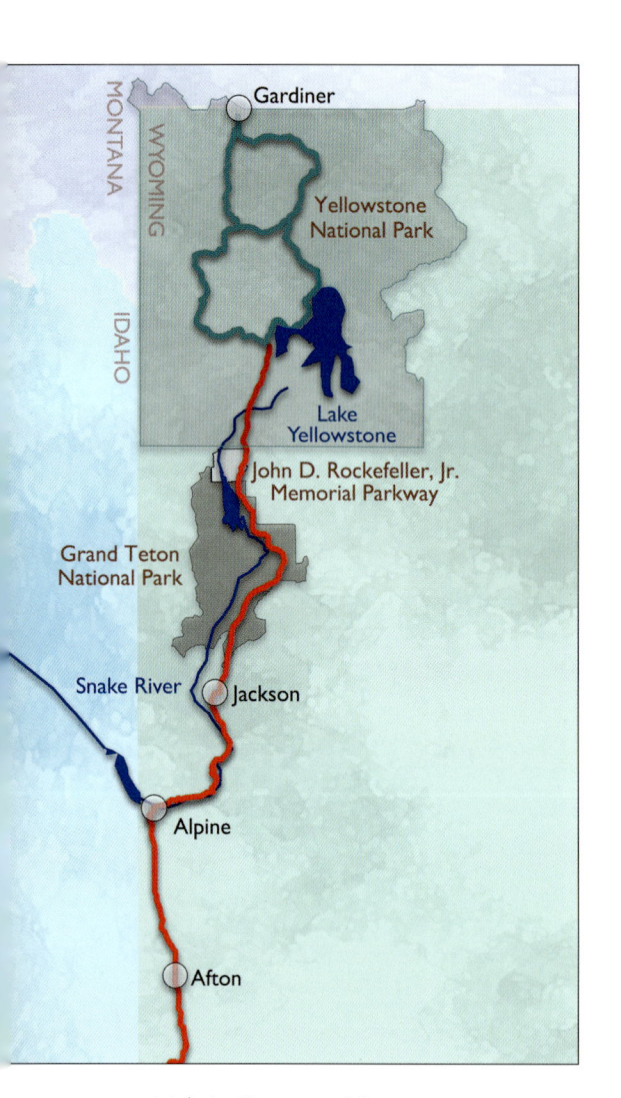

89 through northern Utah, Idaho and far western Wyoming as far as Alpine, where the highway met the Snake River.

At Alpine, Rishel's 1927 map directed motorists back over the Idaho border and into Jackson via the Teton Pass. The treacherous 8,500-foot mountain track required driving fortitude in the short summer months it was clear of snow. Depression-era relief funding helped realize the long-anticipated, expensive road from Alpine to Jackson up the Snake River Canyon. As the road was being constructed, the Utah and Idaho state roads commissions campaigned at the 1936 American Association of State Highway Officials (AASHO) meeting to officially extend U.S. 89 northward from Spanish Fork, Utah, to Jackson, Wyoming, via Bear Lake and Star Valley. Wyoming's highway officials proposed an alternate route for U.S. 89 through Evanston and Hoback Canyon; AASHO took no action. By 1938, Utah and Idaho officials had convinced the far western Wyoming communities to break with their own state highway department and support the Utah/Idaho proposal, which AASHO then approved, bringing Highway 89 to the southern entrance of Yellowstone National Park.

Star Valley

As Highway 89 climbs northward from Montpelier, Idaho, it leaves the Great Basin watershed. Crossing into the headwaters of the Salt River, the road reaches the Snake and Columbia rivershed complex, which drains the northwestern slopes of the Continental Divide to the Pacific Ocean. High sagebrush valleys separate mountain ranges heavily mantled with aspen and conifer forests. Trappers exploited the mountain streams for nearly 40 years before Frederick W. Lander surveyed an Oregon Trail short-cut through the upper Salt River Valley corridor in 1857. Built the following year, it was the only part of the Emigrant Trail constructed with government funds. The Lander Road saved Oregon-bound pioneers 100 miles of travel and remained in use until 1912. Highway 89 roughly parallels its route to Afton, Wyoming.

Culturally and historically, Star Valley's string of tiny communities along the Salt River emerged in the late 1870s and 1880s from the Mormon diaspora of the Intermountain West. The growing LDS membership had expanded the range of its new settlements well beyond the Utah territorial boundaries. Many Wyoming residents welcomed Mormon settlements as a means to pass the population threshold test to qualify for statehood. The 1882 anti-polygamy laws also pushed some Mormon families to the Wyoming/Idaho borderlands, where federal agents could not depend on local law enforcement to pursue suspected polygamists across the territorial line.

Star Valley's climate is too cold for most crops, but its rangeland

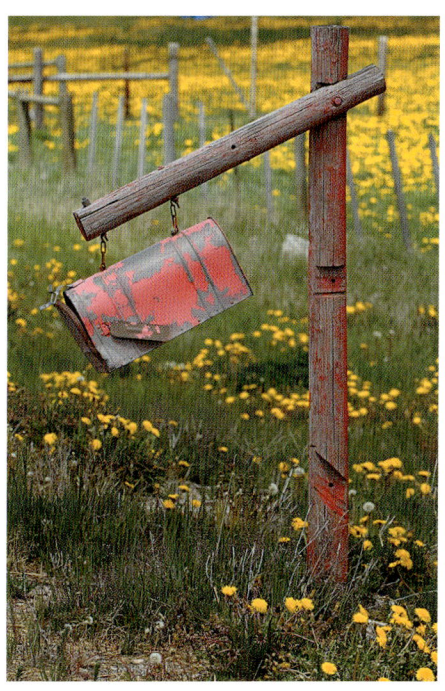

US Highway 89: Wyoming ★ 115

HAND-STACKED HAY: Hay-cutting in the Teton ranching region takes place all summer, after cattle have been moved into mountain pastures. The "beaverslide" is used to stack hay into a water-shedding structure that can protect the grass beneath the surface through many harsh winters. (above)

SNAKE RIVER CANYON: The Snake River Canyon class II and III rapids provide legendary recreation opportunities for rafting, kayaking and fishing. Commercial outfitters pioneered guided trips using surplus World War II military rafts. Today, private citizens and local businesses have combined efforts to form a voluntary organization, in lieu of mandatory user-fees, to fund user services and protect the watershed's ecosystem. (opposite)

provided excellent forage for dairy cattle and local farmers established several cheese-making co-operatives. In 1926, one of the co-ops hired a Swiss immigrant cheese-maker to produce the more profitable Swiss cheese. By 1932, Star Valley was exporting one million pounds of cheese per year. Three cheese-making plants, spaced conveniently throughout the valley when milk was collected by horse and wagon, were replaced in 1949 by a single factory in Thayne. The plant operated almost continuously until 2005, then closed in part because of difficulty in obtaining enough locally produced milk. New ownership in 2008 by an Idaho dairyman may revitalize Star Valley's cheese-making industry.

One of the last settlements in Star Valley, Alpine was established at the confluence of the Salt and Snake rivers, straddling the Wyoming–Idaho border. After the post office opened in 1911, the town's mail was addressed to either Alpine, Idaho, or Alpine, Wyoming, depending on which side the current postmaster happened to reside. The two states built a bridge across the Snake River but argued over highway repair costs. The 1941 Wyoming Federal Writer's Project guide savaged the condition of the shared road, with neither state willing to finance its repair. The Palisades Dam project, begun in 1941 but moth-balled during World War II, was completed in 1957. It created the world's largest earthen dam and also inundated much of the original Alpine townsite. Relocated to the Wyoming side of the border, Alpine today is a community in transition from a rural hamlet to a suburban outpost housing the workers of Jackson, Wyoming.

89 Snowplowing in Jackson Hole

Winter isolation was a fact of life for the early residents of Jackson Hole, with close to 200 inches of snow falling on the valley floor. Mail and freight carriers crossed the Teton Pass in snowshoes or by sleigh into the 1930s. Wyoming invested in rotary plows to keep the roads open: Teton Pass was first cleared for an entire winter in 1937. Highway 89 through the Snake River Canyon, a more practical route to keep open year-round, opened in 1939.

For most of America, World War II shattered the last vestiges of isolation, but actually increased it for Jackson Hole. As Wyoming's residents joined the military or worked in essential agricultural jobs, few workers or funds remained for snowplowing. In the winter of 1943–44, Jackson's residents voted on which of the three main roads into the valley would be plowed. Highway 89 lost out to the road to Rock Springs, which linked the town to the Union Pacific railhead, mail delivery and state government in Cheyenne.

Greater Yellowstone

Yellowstone National Park comprises only a fraction of the Greater Yellowstone Ecosystem (GYE), the largest intact ecosystem in the northern temperate zone. Encompassing both Yellowstone National Park and Grand Teton National Park, the National Elk Refuge, and other federal and private lands, the total land area of GYE exceeds 19 million acres in three states. The GYE concept is used by politicians and land-use managers to frame stewardship policies for goals like protecting grizzly bear habitat or managing elk herds. Highway 89 crosses a finger of the GYE region in the upper Star Valley, although its agricultural and populated valley floor is excluded from most GYE maps, and enters into the heart of the ecosystem as the road ascends the Snake River Canyon.

The 1939 completion of the Highway 89 route through the Grand Canyon of the Snake River not only opened the scenic valley to motorists, its access to the river essentially created a new recreation destination for fishing and boating enthusiasts. Whitewater adventurers had floated the length of the canyon by 1925, but found the return

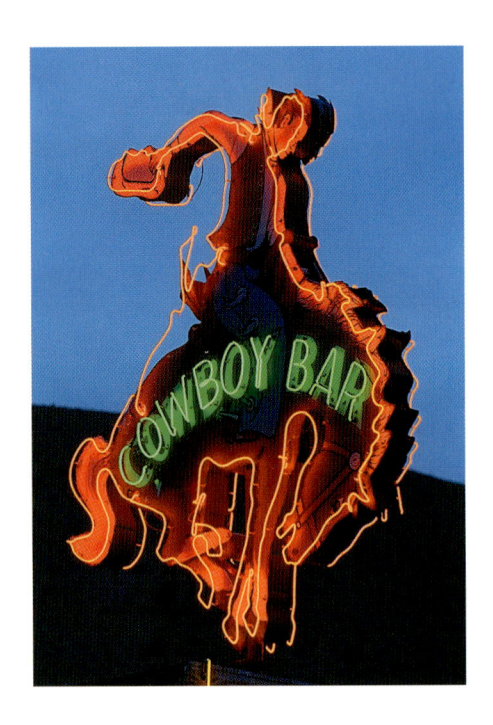

HEAVY LOAD: The National Elk Refuge, adjacent to Jackson, was created in 1912 to provide forage for thousands of elk fenced out of their native winter feeding grounds. Before leaving the refuge each spring, male elk shed their antlers. For decades, the Boy Scouts of Jackson (right) have raised funds by collecting and auctioning the antlers. Antler prices have risen, in part because of the Asian medicine trade and demand for naturally shed antlers for artwork. The refuge partners in the sale and receives 80% of the proceeds of the auction.

COWBOY BAR: Jackson (above)

FAMOUS ARCHES: After decades of deterioration from rough outdoor conditions, the elk antler arches (opposite) at each corner of Jackson's town square needed to be replaced. In 2007 the town of Jackson and its Rotary Club auctioned one of the original arches to raise funds for the rebuilding project. After spirited bidding, the owner of a local motel won the auction with his offer of $51,000. (ooposite)

trip to Jackson via the Teton Pass a greater barrier to commercial trips than the river itself. In the summer of 1940, only a few months after the completion of Highway 89 through the canyon, Clyde Smith pioneered the first commercial float trip and a new Jackson industry. Rafters and kayakers share the river with fishermen in driftboats, casting for a unique subspecies of cutthroat trout known as the Finespotted Snake River cutthroat trout. Today, about 150,000 commercially guided and private users raft the famous rapids – Big Kahuna and Lunch Counter – below the Hoback River confluence.

Jackson, Wyoming

Encircled by federal land, Jackson has mushroomed from an isolated ranching community to a resort destination for the rich and famous, quite unlike any other gateway town to a national park. Dude ranches in the 1920s and the first of three ski resorts in the late 1930s expanded the economic base for tourism beyond the boundaries of Grand Teton National Park. Jackson's early contentious relationship with the National Park Service over the creation of the park led to some unlikely compromises, including the only commercial airport within a national park. Highway 89 itself was moved from the western side of the park (the previous designation followed the road from

Poaching elk for their teeth

The canines of the bull elk, known as "elk tusks," were worn as fashionable gentlemen's accessories and symbols of the influential Benevolent & Protective Order of Elks. The high price of the teeth at the turn of the 20th century led to a wanton slaughtering of bull elk, with the carcasses simply left to rot. The practice so enraged Jackson's citizens in 1906 that they ran a poaching group out of town. The poaching continued: in 1915, "tuskers" killed 5,000 elk in Yellowstone alone. Demand plummeted after the fraternal order banned wearing the teeth as a symbol of membership.

Moose to Jenny Lake and the Jackson Lake Dam) to an all-weather road suitable for heavy commercial traffic. As part of the 1950 agreements to expand Grand Teton National Park, the National Park Service collects no fees from motorists traveling between Jackson and Moran Junction, where U.S. 89 branches from U.S. 26/287.

Luxury resorts, golf courses and an arts community draw millions of tourists to the Jackson Hole area, and in recent decades, induced many to stay. Jackson's population doubled in the 1970s and again in the 1990s, causing land prices to skyrocket. Growth brought a host

US Highway 89: Wyoming ★ 119

SNAKE RIVER: Quaking aspens and cottonwood trees are members of the poplar family and both turn brilliant yellow in autumn. Aspens prefer habitat above 5,000 feet and are found both on the margins of the sagebrush steppe and intermixed conifer forests. Cottonwoods edge the banks of streams and rivers throughout the west. The Snake River (above) meanders an ancestral alluvial plain built up when its hydraulics system carried massive sediment loads produced by melting glaciers.

SPARRING PRACTICE: Bull elk shed their antlers in early spring, before leaving the winter feeding grounds at the National Elk Refuge. (opposite, below)

FISHING FAIRY: Jackson Lake was dammed in the 1910s to provide irrigation water to Idaho farmers, interrupting the free flow of the Snake River from its headwaters in Yellowstone National Park. Traditional dories launch at the base of the dam, drifting fishermen through superb trout waters. Jessica and her family were fishing on the banks of the river; Jessica chose her sportswear herself. (opposite, above)

of issues the town's newest residents had tried to leave behind: traffic congestion, sprawl and affordable housing for the region's workforce. With 97 percent of Teton County's land in the federal domain, Jackson's challenge is to integrate future development with its historic character into a new kind of livable Western destination town.

National Elk Refuge

Summer visitors traveling between Jackson and Grand Teton National Park could easily confuse the National Elk Refuge with a bird sanctuary. At the refuge overlook on the edge of Jackson, plenty of ducks, geese and the occasional trumpeter swan fly over its meadows and dabble in its ponds, but not a single elk can be seen grazing on its 20,000 acres.

Winter transforms the vista, as snow in the higher elevations drives thousands of elk in search of forage into the Jackson Hole valley from southern Yellowstone National Park, Grand Teton National Park and the Bridger-Teton National Forest. Reports of starving elk, blocked from their traditional winter grazing lands by homesteaders, reached a flash point in the harsh winters of 1908–09 and 1909–10, when as many as 20,000 elk starved in the valley. Ranchers raised money to buy hay, the state of Wyoming contributed emergency funds, and conservationist and photographer Stephen N. Leek's images of the elk herd helped propel Congress to create the National Elk Refuge in 1912.

After the fall rut, elk herds trail mature females down from the high country on established migration routes. The region's hunters harvest about 20 percent of the herd each year, with a target population of 7,500 animals wintering at the refuge. Refuge staff supplement the natural winter forage about 70 days each year, at a cost of about $40 per elk. Several hundred bison also winter at the refuge, as do the GYE predators: coyote, wolf and the rare, elusive mountain lion. Once snow conditions permit, the public can take guided tours of elk feeding grounds in horse-drawn sleighs.

Bull elk, who remain in bachelor groups for most of the year, shed their massive antlers in early spring before leaving the refuge. By midsummer, they have grown replacements, sometimes at a rate of more than an inch a day. A mature male's six-point antlers weigh between 10 and 12 pounds. For more than 50 years, the National Elk Refuge has partnered with Jackson's Boy Scouts to gather shed antlers and auction them at a day-long event in Jackson's town square. Naturally shed antlers draw a premium for high-end decorative crafts and Asian medicines, with a matched set selling for hundreds of dollars. The refuge funds infrastructure and habitat projects with its 80 percent share of the auction proceeds.

Grand Teton National Park

"If you have ever stood at Jenny Lake and looked across to Cascade Canyon weaving its sinuous way toward the summit of the Tetons, you will know the joy of being in a sacred place, designed by God to be protected forever." (Horace Albright, Creating the National Park Service*)*

During the summer of 1916, in the midst of their battle with Congress to create the National Park Service administrative structure, Stephen Mather and Horace Albright toured Yellowstone National Park with proponents of a proposed "Park-to-Park Highway." Albright badgered his boss, Mather, to visit the Teton Range on the tour. Albright wrote later that he immediately wanted to include it within Yellowstone's boundaries for its exemplary glacial geologic features, saying to himself on that first visit, "Now this is a national park!"

The Teton Range soars 7,000 feet above the Jackson Hole basin. Three separate glacial periods chiseled mountain peaks into spires and scoured canyons. Ice, flowing under the pressure of gravity and its own extreme weight, transported the debris. Jumbled moraines were left behind as the ice retreated, forming catch basins for a string of clear blue lakes at the feet of the mountains. The Snake River, originating in southern Yellowstone National Park, parallels the Teton Range, stopping briefly to fill its largest lake. Below the Jackson Lake outlet, the Snake River winds across Jackson Hole's sagebrush steppe and grasslands; the spacious landscape is a breathtaking counterpoint to the lofty skyline.

In the intervening four decades since Yellowstone National Park's southern boundary had been fixed, ranchers and farmers had taken up land claims throughout Jackson Hole. Idaho farmers with lands downstream on the Snake River had built a dam on Jackson Lake and held rights to the stored water. Private property interests, the inter-agency rivalry with National Forest jurisdiction over the surrounding timbered mountain slopes, and a Wyoming political current that railed against federal intrusion into local land-use policies, thwarted Albright's and others' efforts to enlarge Yellowstone National Park for two decades.

Opposition from Idaho representatives stalled a bill in the 1918 Congress, although President Woodrow Wilson withdrew 600,000 acres in the Teton National Forest from future homesteading claims. As Acting Director in 1918, Albright sought out influential Jackson residents, including newspaperman Dick Winger, to encourage support for expanding Yellowstone's boundaries to the south, despite Mather's orders to back-burner the project until after the nation recovered from World War I.

Albright, promoted to Superintendent of Yellowstone in 1919, watched his dream edge further away over the years as land prices rose in Jackson Hole. In 1924, one of the wealthiest and most powerful men in America, John D. Rockefeller, Jr., and three of his sons toured several western national parks, including Yellowstone. The park superintendents on the Rockefeller itinerary were given absolute instructions not to discuss any park service business with the philanthropist. Traveling incognito, the family toured the park by automobile; Albright encouraged a lunch stop at Jackson Lake, hoping to pique Rockefeller's curiosity about the Tetons without disobeying orders.

A few weeks later, Rockefeller wrote to Albright to thank him for his hospitality and to comment on the unsightly debris on the roadsides of Yellowstone National Park from previous construction projects. Albright replied that, while he was unhappy with the mess, Congress had never appropriated a sufficient budget for Yellowstone's road needs, and he did not have funds for clean-up crews. The men exchanged more letters, and Albright proposed that Rockefeller fund a test project to see how much it would cost to clear the roadsides. Rockefeller sent Albright $12,000 for the initial work, which later grew into $50,000 and a four-year project. The success of the project encouraged roadside clean-up in other parks and eventually a National Park Service-wide policy to budget for roadside restoration in all future road-building projects. More importantly, a unique partnership between two men was born.

Rockefeller, his wife Abby and his younger sons returned to Yellowstone National Park in 1926, and Albright gave them a personal Yellowstone tour. This time, he included the Jackson Hole area. Progress on the roadside clean-up inside Yellowstone pleased the Rockefellers; the conditions beyond the park's boundaries did not. Billboards competed for attention, telephone poles crossed between the road and mountains, and abandoned structures marred the view. Seeing his chance, Albright shared his dream with the couple at a campfire that night: to raise funds to buy out the local owners and protect the whole valley. As night descended on the Tetons, the Rockefellers said nothing.

The following winter, Albright called on Rockefeller in his New York office. He was stunned to learn that the philanthropist intended to purchase all of

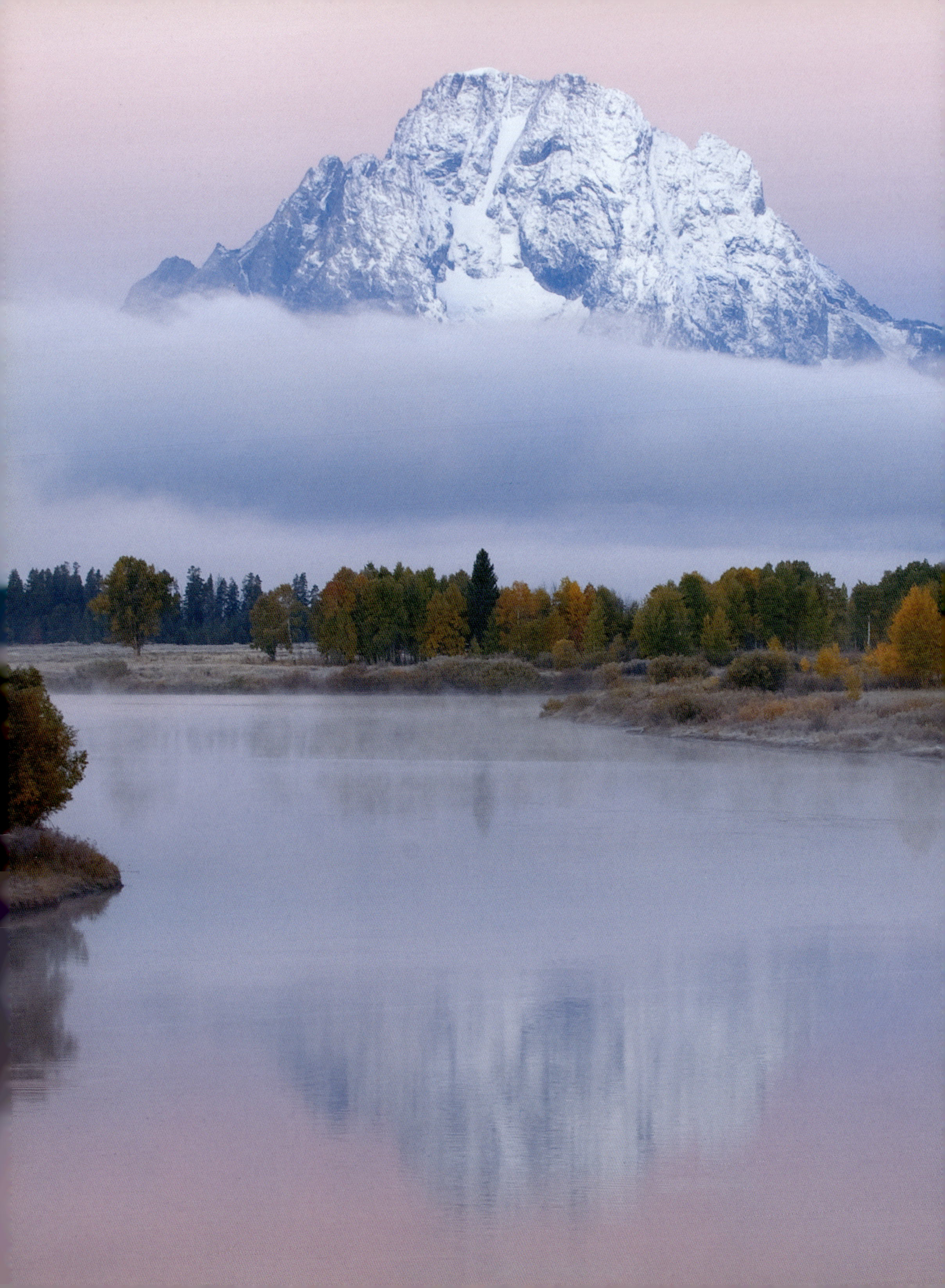

the land that Albright had proposed and hold them until Congress authorized the National Park Service to accept them as a gift. Because of local opposition and the risk of price gouging, Rockefeller made anonymous purchases by setting up a corporation, rumored in Jackson to be a cattle company. By 1930, the Snake River Land Company had bought more than 30,000 acres at a price of over $1.4 million.

Local opposition to national park status for the Grand Teton/Snake River complex outlasted Albright's service, both as Yellowstone Superintendent and as Stephen Mather's successor as the second director of the National Park Service. Loss of taxable lands in a poor county in the midst of the Depression worried local residents, as did the threat that additional federal regulation, increased tourism and loss of grazing lands would impinge on Jackson residents' lifestyle and values. Congress approved a 1929 bill to create the first boundaries of Grand Teton National Park, which protected the Teton Range itself and the smaller lakes at its base, but excluded the land adjacent to the Snake River and even the eastern shores of Jackson Lake.

Rockefeller announced his role in the Snake River Land Company and his intention to transfer the land to the NPS in 1930. Various legislative efforts to expand Grand Teton National Park and accept Rockefeller's donation failed throughout the 1930s. As Rockefeller's philanthropic patience reached its limits, President Franklin D. Roosevelt created the Jackson Hole National Monument in 1943 by executive declaration. Taken by surprise, Congress first tried to rescind the declaration (which Roosevelt vetoed), then attached provisions to the Interior Department's appropriation bill to prevent federal funds from being spent to administer the unit. Finally in 1950, the full enabling legislation was passed and Rockefeller's donated lands were incorporated into the new boundaries of Grand Teton National Park.

In 1972, the U.S. Congress designated a 24,000-acre corridor of land on either side of Highway 89 between Grand Teton and Yellowstone national parks as the John D. Rockefeller, Jr. Memorial Parkway. In addition to the Jackson Hole area donations, Rockefeller made important gifts to the nation in support of Acadia, Virgin Islands and the Great Smoky Mountains national parks. In 2001, his son, Laurance (who rode with his father and Albright on the 1924 and 1926 tours), donated the last 1,106-acre Rockefeller-owned in-holding to Grand Teton National Park.

Yellowstone National Park
What makes the Yellowstone region unique is not the volcanic eruption that ripped open a caldera 40 miles across. Violent volcanism exists around the globe. However, it is usually found near coastlines where an oceanic continental plate is actively diving beneath a neighboring section of the earth's crust. In Yellowstone, 50 million years had passed since plate tectonics had uplifted western Wyoming and Montana. Yet, only about two million years ago, the Yellowstone Plateau Volcanic Field exploded in the Rocky Mountains, in the heart of the continent.

Heat from the still-active volcanic field provides half of the necessary conditions for Yellowstone National Park's fantastic geothermal features. The other requirement is met by abundant precipitation, triggered when wet storm systems collide with the Rocky Mountains, which percolates into the groundwater, only to be thrust out to the surface as geysers, fumaroles and hot springs. More than 10,000 geothermal features are found in Yellowstone National Park, by far the greatest concentration in the world.

Yellowstone's iconic geysers may draw in crowds (more than three million people visited the park in 2007), but they compete for star billing with the park's many other scenic wonders: North America's largest mountain lake (Yellowstone Lake), a waterfall (Lower Yellowstone Falls) twice the height of Niagara Falls, and abundant wildlife, including the lower 48 states' largest population of grizzly bear. Free-roaming bison herds, regenerated from a remnant population of only four dozen, give the park's Lamar Valley the title, "North America's Serengeti."

Had Wyoming already achieved statehood in 1872, the effort to preserve the wonders of Yellowstone as a national park might have taken a very different trajectory. The Yosemite valley had already been set aside in 1864 by President Abraham Lincoln, but was turned over to California as a state park

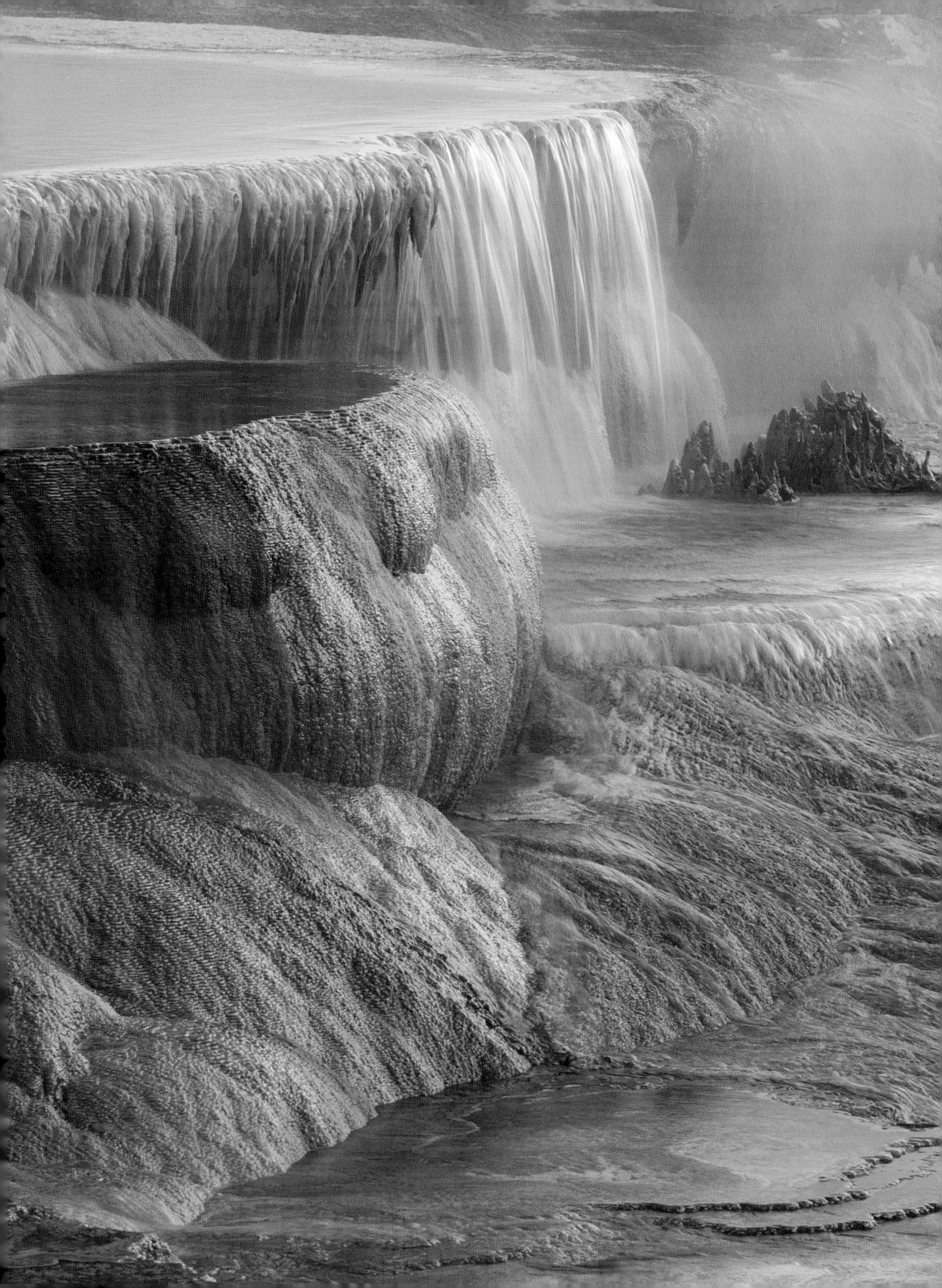

(it was returned to the federal government when Yosemite became a national park in 1890). President Andrew Jackson reserved the land that became Hot Springs National Park even earlier, in 1832. Yellowstone lore tells how a group of influential Montana businessmen and officials, making a month's reconnaissance through the region in 1870, conceived of the idea to create the world's first national park at a campfire beside the Madison River. Whether the fireside conversation actually took place is not recorded, but on their return, the men began to campaign to preserve Yellowstone's lands as a public park.

The audacity of the idea to create Yellowstone National Park was in its scale: 3,468 square miles (greater than the combined size of Delaware and Rhode Island) would not be available to land-hungry settlers. Never before had so much valuable timber, grazing and mining resources been withdrawn from private use. Yet, advocates for Yellowstone's wilderness soon began to suggest that the park wasn't big enough. After an 1882 visit, Civil War General Philip Sheridan argued Yellowstone's size needed to be doubled if it were to function as a game reserve. *Saturday Evening Post* writer Emerson Hough, who is credited with the phrase "Greater Yellowstone" in a 1917 article, also proposed to double the Yellowstone National Park acreage and save Jackson Hole from logging and mining interests.

Congress appropriated minimal public funds in the park's first decade to patrol Yellowstone or to provide roads, trails and lodging, although early superintendents managed to install signage and construct rudimentary roads to the park's most prominent features. From the 1880s, the Northern Pacific Railway made infrastructure investments, most spectacularly the Old Faithful Inn, to accommodate its passengers arriving via its transcontinental line across Montana.

The U.S. Army Corps of Engineers brought funds and expertise in 1883 to build the park's roads, and in 1886 the U.S. Cavalry took over day-to-day administration of the park to protect it from vandalism and poaching. Lt. Dan C. Kingman laid out Yellowstone National Park's "Grand Loop" road to the park's major waypoints. In the process, Kingman established standards for road-building in the national parks, writing that the roads should "have something of the solid, durable and substantial quality that usually characterized the works constructed by the national government." Lt. Hiram Chittenden continued Kingman's road building outline, addressing one of the greatest engineering challenges in the Grand Loop: bridging the Yellowstone River above its upper falls. He kept crews working through the 1903 winter to complete the Mount Washburn Road over 8,859 foot Dunraven Pass, and designed the park's iconic north entrance arch.

After the creation of the National Park Service in 1916, and with the demands of World War I, the army was persuaded to return

THE TETON RANGE: Grand Teton National Park (pages 122–3)

MOUNT MORAN: Sunrise above the oxbow, a quiet arm of the Snake River, home to osprey, moose, bald eagles and beaver. In this haven, young otters eat fish held like an ice cream cone and surf in riffles. The stillness of an autumn dawn morning is broken by bugling elk or distant coyotes howling a pack wake-up song. (page 124)

CANARY SPRINGS: Travertine terraces at Mammoth Hot Springs, near the northern entrance of Yellowstone National Park (opposite)

BISON CALF: Bison calves are born in April or May and weigh 40 to 50 pounds. After about three months, they begin to lose their first, reddish-tan coat, fully transitioning to dark brown by about six months of age. (above)

SUMMER SPECTACLE: In 2006, over 15 million people visited the seven national parks served by Highway 89. Yellowstone National Park alone attracted 3 million people, with about 85 percent visiting the Old Faithful area. (above) The crowds peak on summer holidays, and can reach 25,000 people per day.

WINTER PLUME: Old Faithful's steam column rises high in the cold winter air at Yellowstone National Park. (opposite)

day-to-day command of the park to the Department of the Interior. The transfer also relieved the Corps of Engineers of its responsibility for the park's roads. Immediately, Stephen Mather faced an imperative to improve Yellowstone's roads for motor vehicles. Lacking the expertise within the park service, Mather negotiated an agreement with another new federal agency, the Bureau of Public Roads (BPR). The National Park Service would obtain funding from Congress and the BPR would provide road-building expertise, in concert with the NPS Landscape Engineering Office. The agreement did not go so far as to add Yellowstone's Grand Loop into the BPR's primary highway numbering system; U.S. 89 breaks off at the park's southern entrance and recommences at the northern gates in Gardiner, Montana.

Over the years, roads in Yellowstone National Park were improved, but generally retained the original shape cast by the Corps of Engineers. In 1918, Acting Director Horace Albright saw no need to build more roads:

"For the time being and probably the foreseeable future, Yellowstone would get along just fine with General Chittenden's army roads. Improve them yes, but we wouldn't encourage any more. All the wondrous sights were on Chittenden's loop route, which left the vast majority of the park in wilderness."

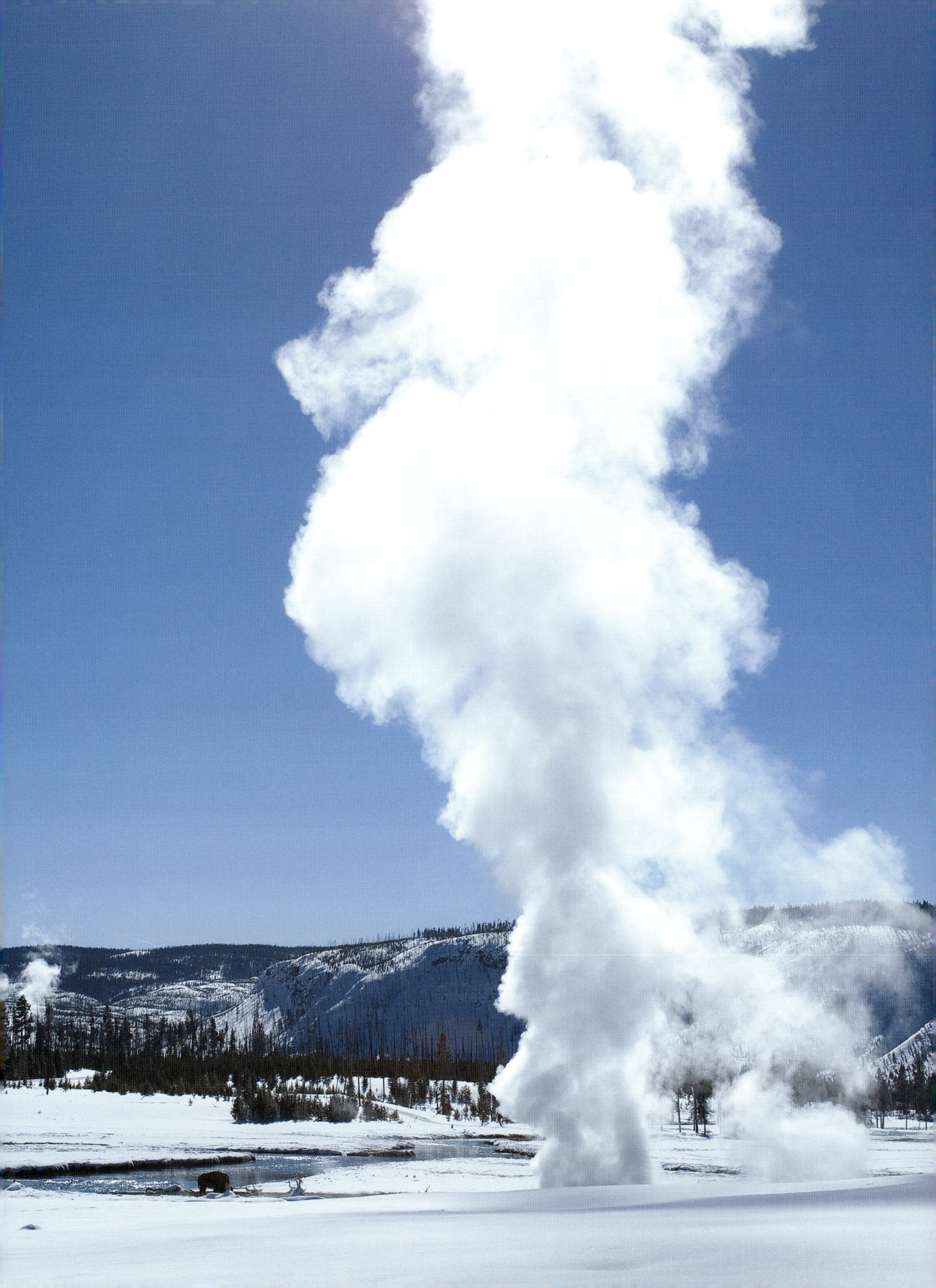

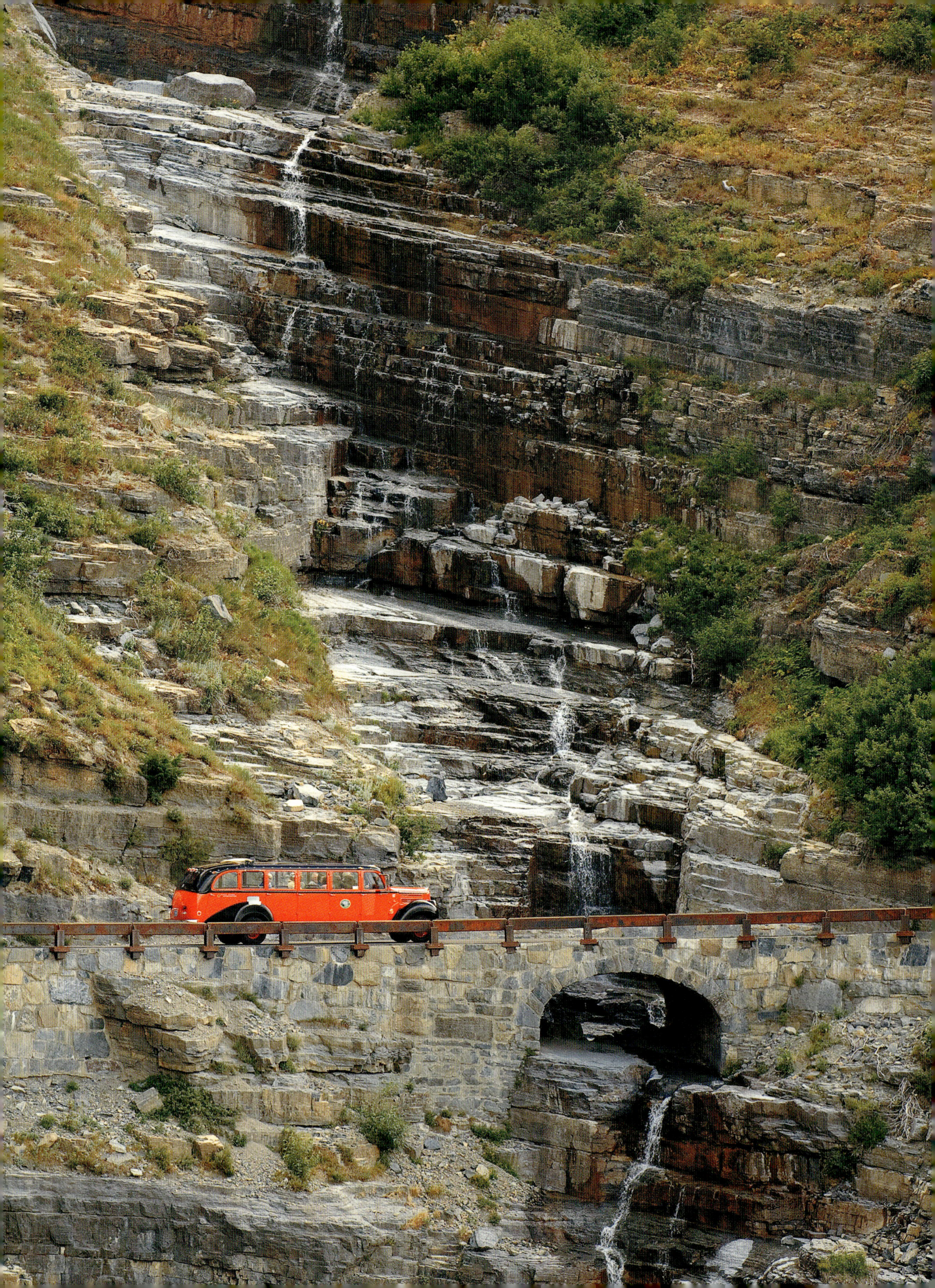

The Park-to-Park Highway
★ ★ ★ Gardiner to Piegan, Montana ★ ★ ★ ★ ★ ★ ★

By 1920, named highways and trails crisscrossed America. National parks featured highly in many of the transcontinental routes, like the Yellowstone Trail and the Ocean-to-Ocean Highway in Arizona. The Park-to-Park (P2P) Highway Association turned the strategy upside-down, promoting a circle tour of 12 western parks (including Yellowstone, Zion and Grand Canyon national parks) as destinations themselves, rather than scenic stopovers en route to somewhere else. National Park Service Director Stephen Mather gave early support to the Park-to-Park Highway Association, hosting them in Yellowstone National Park on a 1916 pathfinding trip, and sending NPS representation on the entire 1920 dedication tour.

From Denver, the 6,000-mile Park-to-Park Highway stopped first at Colorado's Rocky Mountain National Park, then steered motorists across Wyoming to the eastern entrance of Yellowstone National Park. From Yellowstone's northern gateway, the association recommended the Yellowstone–Glacier–Banff Highway route to Glacier National Park, which was later adopted as Montana's segment of U.S. 89.

Montanans promoted two competing trails between the parks. The Geysers-to-Glaciers Highway directed motorists through Helena to the western side of Glacier National Park. The Yellowstone–Glacier–Banff Highway (also known as the YGB or Yellowstone–Glacier Bee-line Highway) ran through Great Falls. The Bee-line, which was promoted as the more direct route between the two parks, channeled motorists to Glacier's eastern entrance.

GOING-TO-THE-SUN ROAD: During the Depression, the White Motor Company built 500 touring coaches for use in the national parks, including the Grand Circle of Zion, Bryce Canyon and the Grand Canyon, as well as Yellowstone and Glacier national parks. After 60 years in service, Glacier's original fleet of red buses (opposite) was reconditioned by Ford Motor Company and converted to run on clean-burning propane fuel. In Glacier, the driver/guides were known as "Jammers" for their noisy, gear-jamming driving techniques while summiting the Going-to-the-Sun Road.

ROCKY MOUNTAIN BIGHORN SHEEP: Glacier National Park (above)

The Yellowstone Trail
The Park-to-Park Highway traveled in reverse the final miles of one the nation's oldest "good road" efforts, the Yellowstone Trail. Primarily a route from Minneapolis to Seattle, the Yellowstone Trail culminated in a 56-mile spur from Livingston to the park's grand entrance

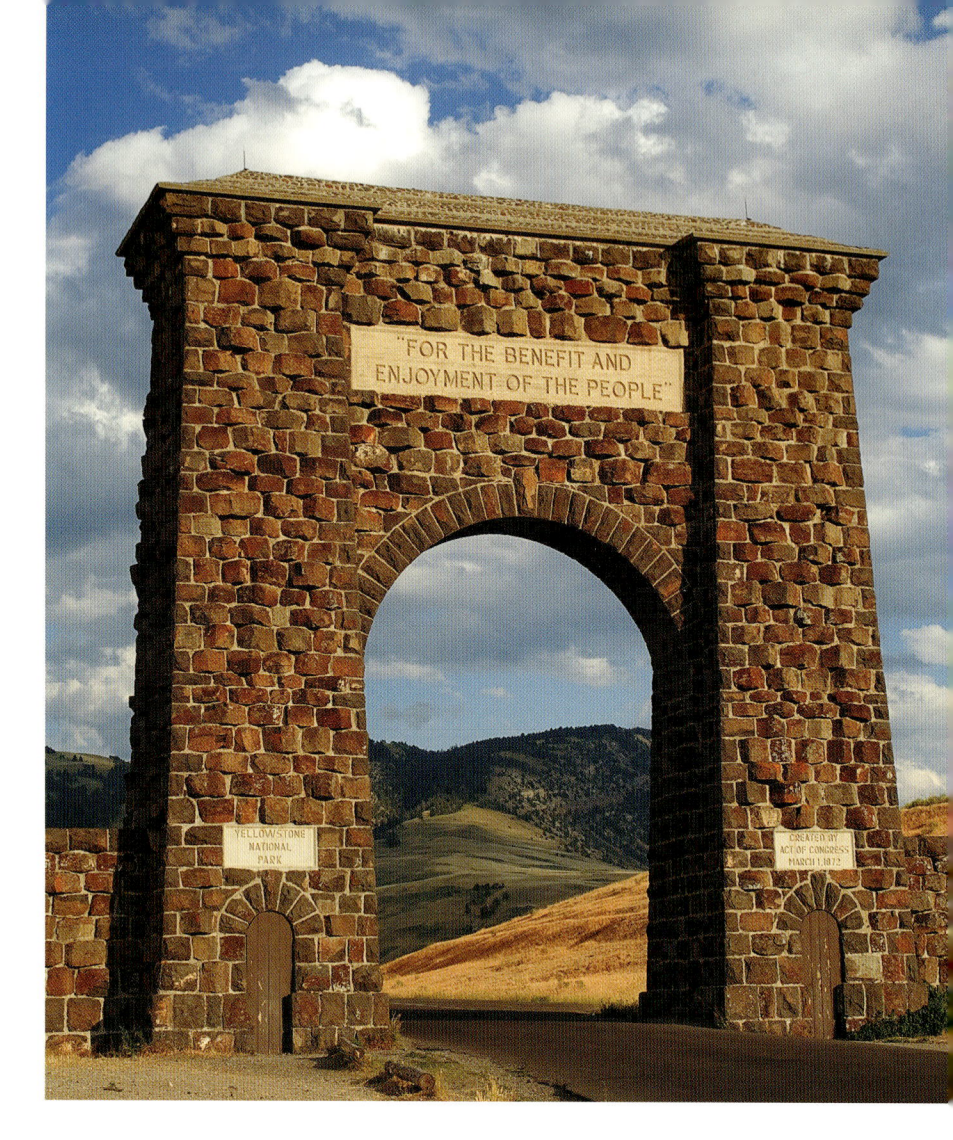

arch in Gardiner, Montana. Blazed with a black arrow painted on a yellow background, much of the highway was graded and graveled by volunteers on organized trail-building days, although convict labor helped improve the Livingston to Gardiner segment.

Within months of the establishment of Yellowstone National Park, Montana businessmen sought federal funding to build a road to its north entrance. When they failed, entrepreneur James George cleared a route through the narrow mountain canyon and set up a tollgate in 1873. His lucrative monopoly lasted for a decade, until the Northern Pacific Railway exercised their right of way to force access through the canyon. "Yankee Jim" held off the railway surveyors at gunpoint, the dispute landed in court, and eventually the railway agreed to build George a replacement road through "his" canyon. He collected tolls until the county took over the road, which later became part of the official Yellowstone Trail. In the 1920s, the road was added to the federal highway system and reconstructed on the east side of Yankee Jim Canyon. Though not maintained, segments of the abandoned Yellowstone Trail can still be seen from Highway 89.

Just as the trail and highway associations vied for transcontinental motorists, by 1920 six railway companies promoted competing

132 ★ THE PARK-TO-PARK HIGHWAY

east-west lines across the country. Highway 89 transects three of the six lines in Montana. Armed with an 1864 Congressional charter and land grant of 40 million acres (larger than Georgia or Illinois), the Northern Pacific Railway survived near-bankruptcy and a hostile takeover, taking 19 years to pound its final, golden spike in 1883. That same year, the Northern Pacific began a spur line from Livingston to Yellowstone National Park, carrying 20,000 park-bound passengers in its first year of service. Livingston became a regional center for the Northern Pacific, with its largest roundhouse between Minnesota and the West Coast. Gardiner grew up as the nation's first gateway town to a national park. Saloons and other, less wholesome, entertainments provided tourists with amenities lacking in the park itself. The sidewalks of Gardiner's prime business real estate literally front the park boundary, resulting in a curious main street approach devoid of buildings on one side. Though the last regular passenger train left Gardiner in 1948, the wheels of transcontinental freight trains still rumble through Livingston's depot, designed by the same architecture firm as New York's Grand Central Station.

ROOSEVELT ARCH: President Theodore Roosevelt ended a two week vacation in Yellowstone National Park by ceremonially troweling mortar for the corner stone of the park's northern entry arch. (opposite).

THE EMPIRE: Downtown Livingston glows at night with an abundance of well-preserved vintage neon signs. (left)

ROAD-SIDE SHRINE: A Marian shrine (below) frames the Absaroka Mountains near Emigrant.

MONTANA
ELEV' Co.
MONTANA ELEVATOR CO.
SAPPHIRE FLOUR
CERETANA FEED

Montana's Mining Country

After crossing the Yellowstone River outside of Livingston, Highway 89 courses through the margins of Montana's storied mining districts. Across western Montana, a series of boom-to-bust cycles brought wealth to the pockets of a few and littered the countryside with ghost towns. A gold-mining town like Diamond City, 30 miles west of White Sulphur Springs, could go from a handful of mining claims to 10,000 residents within five years, and just as quickly dwindle away. Between Livingston and White Sulphur Springs, the Castle Mountain silver mining district boasted 2,000 residents in the 1880s. The mines around Neihart on the Kings Hill section of Highway 89 fared better. With a variety of mineral resources beyond silver and lead, and a rail spur to lower production costs, it was profitable to mine ore with lower concentrations of silver.

At Ringling, Highway 89 crosses the remnants of the Milwaukee Road, the last of the great transcontinental railroad projects. The Chicago, Milwaukee, St. Paul and Pacific Railroad didn't even begin building westward until 1906, long after the other five lines were completed. But by 1909, the Milwaukee Road was competing head-to-head with Montana's other railways. To make up for its shorter but more challenging and costly grades, the railway installed the nation's

MONTANA'S CASTLE: Homesteader Byron Roger Sherman had silver mining interests in Neihart and operated a stage line between White Sulphur Springs and Neihart and Castle. His home in White Sulphur Springs, known as the Castle (above), was completed in 1892 at a cost of $36,000. In 1967, the subsequent owners donated the structure to Meagher County Historical Society for use as a museum in commemoration of the town's centennial.

GRAIN ELEVATOR: Wilsall (opposite)

FIRE FINDER: From the Porphyry tower (above), a nine-year veteran fire lookout demonstrates the use of an Osborne Fire Finder (top) to precisely locate smoke columns in the surrounding forest.

ROADSIDE RELIC: Abandoned mining structure alongside Highway 89 near Neihart (opposite)

first long-distance electric freight line from Harlowton, Montana, to Avery, Idaho.

The entire town of Ringling relocated to take advantage of the new transportation hub where the White Sulphur Springs & Yellowstone Park Railway met the Milwaukee Road's tracks. New Dorsey had already moved once, and in the second relocation, the residents renamed the town for circus owner John Ringling, an important local landholder. The town hoped Ringling would establish winter-quarters for the circus in the area; instead, Ringling installed one of the world's largest dairy barns near White Sulphur Springs. As its competitors formed mergers into much larger lines, the Milwaukee Road failed and declared bankruptcy in 1977. While the tracks through Ringling have been pulled up, the shuttered depot still stands in the village center.

Like many who to tried to make a start in Montana's gold mines, James Brewer took up ranching in the Smith River valley. Learning that native people used a nearby hot springs for medicinal purposes, he soon moved his operation and opened Brewer's Springs. Weary miners paid 75 cents for a bath (not including whiskey). When Brewer sold the springs in 1876, the federal postmaster insisted on a new name for the town: White Sulphur Springs was the accepted substitute. Later owners added a hotel and shipped bottled mineral water across the region. Hotel guests at the 1891 Christmas dinner could choose from fresh oysters, white tail or black tail venison, quail on toast, three kinds of pie and lemon ice cream. Today, a modern

136 ★ THE PARK-TO-PARK HIGHWAY

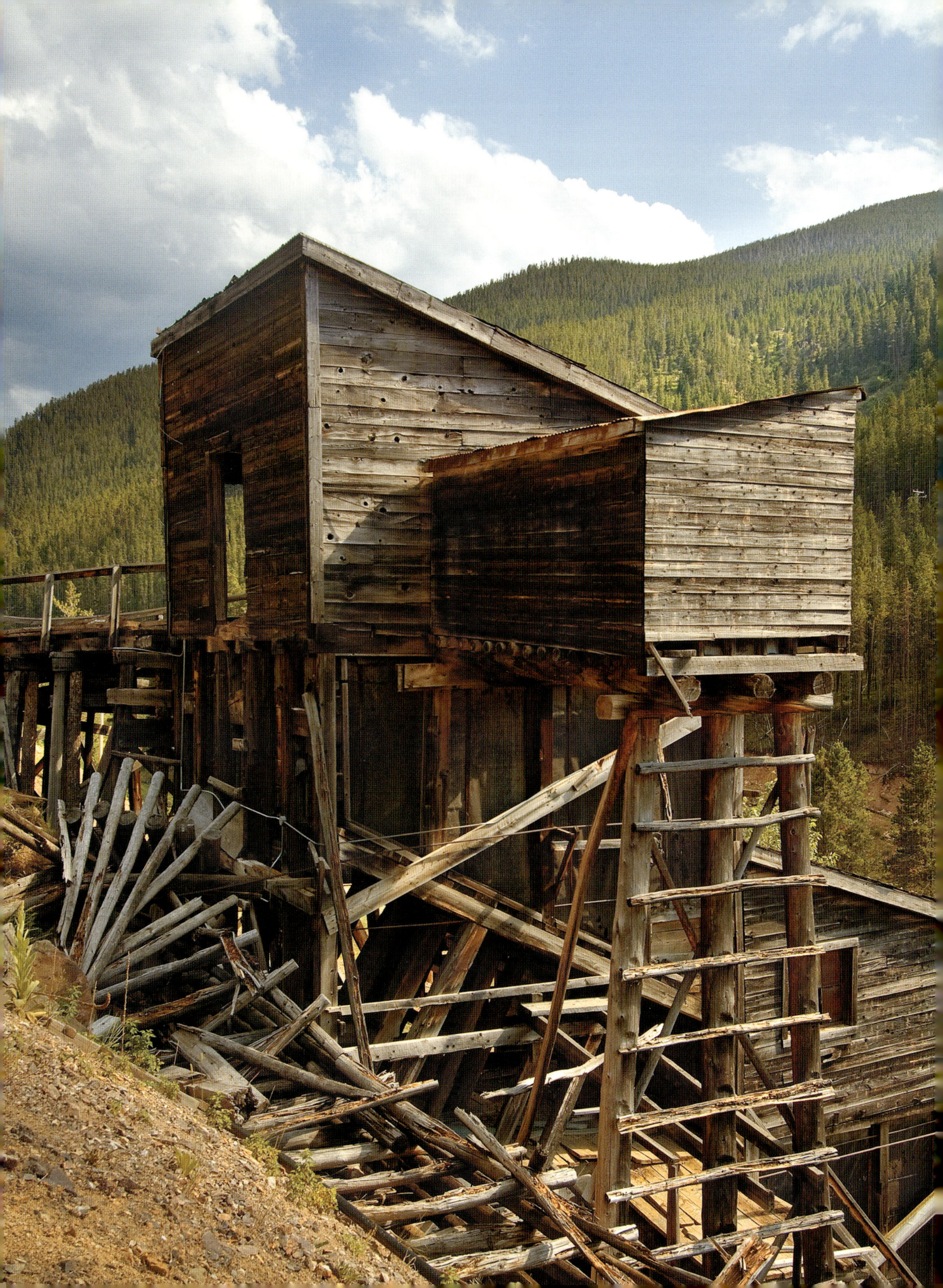

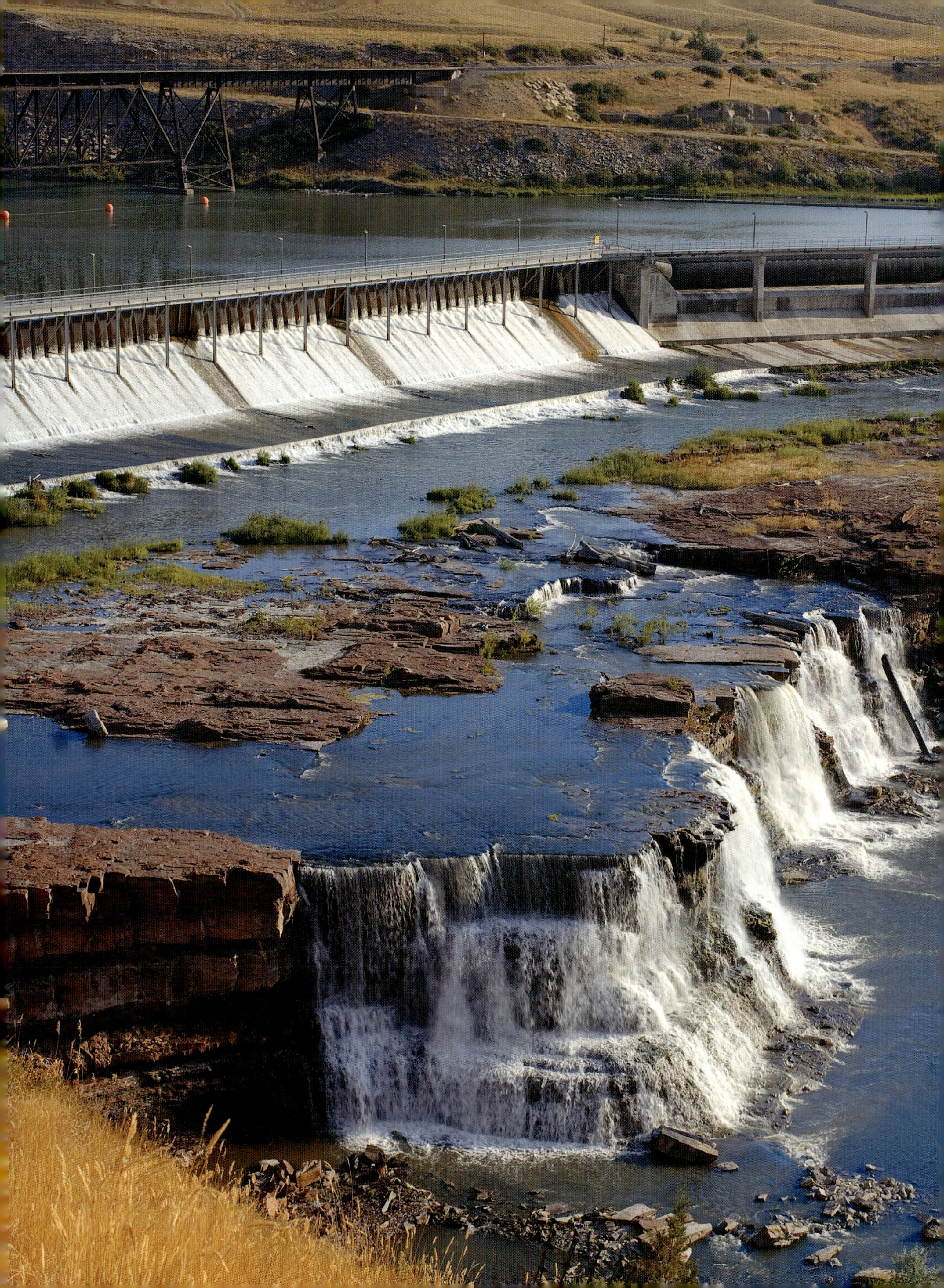

motel with indoor and outdoor pools hosts a stream of skiers and snowmobilers visiting the nearby Kings Hill winter recreation area.

Kings Hill Scenic Byway

As Highway 89 leaves Yellowstone, the Continental Divide trends westward. The Rocky Mountains form the lower border between Montana and Idaho, then loop back to the north, meeting the highway again near Choteau. The mountain ranges to the east of the divide–Absarokas, Crazies and Little Belts — have more recent, complex geologic origins, characterized by igneous intrusions into ancient, sometimes Precambrian, basement rock. The Absarokas (east of Gardiner) erupted about 50 million years ago, while volcanic flows in the Crazy Mountains (Shields River Valley) cooled below

RAINBOW FALLS: Beneath Rainbow Dam, the falls (opposite) drop 47 feet on the Missouri River. A partnership of government agencies, private enterprises and citizen volunteers in Great Falls has built 30 miles of pedestrian and biking trails linking the dams on the Missouri River.

STRETCHING DEER HIDE: On the banks of the Missouri River, visitors to the Lewis and Clark Interpretive Center in Great Falls, Montana, get a first-hand experience (left) at preparing skins for clothing. The physical demands on the Corps of Discovery wore out their clothing in a matter of days. If no local native tribes were nearby to trade for replacements, the explorers had to stop long enough to make their own.

MILWAUKEE ROAD DEPOT: Colorful tile mosaics emblazoned on the tower distinguishes the Chicago Milwaukee and St. Paul Passenger Depot (above) from the Great Northern station (its clock tower is 15 feet higher). Both depots were completed in 1909 to handle the thousands of settlers streaming into Montana's prairies; both buildings have been converted to office space.

US HIGHWAY 89: MONTANA ★ 139

EAR MOUNTAIN: Though not its tallest peak, Ear Mountain (above) has one of the most distinctive and recognizable profiles along the Rocky Mountain Front.

TETON COUNTY COURTHOUSE: One goal of the 1926 primary highway system was to connect every county courthouse in the 48 states with a road that could be traveled at 35 miles per hour. Highway 89 passes many regal courthouses of that era, including those of Santa Cruz (Nogales, Arizona), Yavapai (Prescott, Arizona), Piute (Junction, Utah) and Bear Lake (Paris, Idaho) counties. However, only in Teton County (Choteau, Montana) does the highway circle the courthouse. In 1926, after a series of accidents left car wrecks strewn on the lawn, Teton County installed signs directing motorists to travel around the courthouse in a counterclockwise direction. (opposite)

the surface, forming (among other features) a single, spectacular dike in the southern part of the range. The Little Belts (White Sulphur Springs to Belt) are dotted with laccoliths, pools of magma trapped between sedimentary rock layers that bulged upward in the cooling process. Between the summit of Kings Hill pass and Neihart, an unusual pink and green Precambrian rock appears in road cuts, pinto diorite, in which the Neihart silver-lead was discovered.

Improving the Kings Hill Road between White Sulphur Springs and Great Falls was a top priority of the Yellowstone–Glacier Bee-line Association; Scott Leavitt of Great Falls was one of its greatest champions. At various and sometimes overlapping intervals, Leavitt served as president of both the YGB and the P2P Associations, as well as superintendent of the Jefferson National Forest (which included the Kings Hill area) and as Montana Congressman from 1923–33. The highway's barrier–physical and financial–was the 7,393 foot ascent over the Little Belt Mountains, at the time Montana's highest highway pass. Improvements to support heavy vehicle traffic were essential to ensure that the auto stage lines and private motorists traveling between the parks would not divert to the competing Geysers-to-Glaciers Highway.

Once constructed, the local communities took a vigorous part in opening the highway as early as possible each season. Crews from

White Sulphur Springs shoveled snow at the pass (the Helena Daily Independent reported that a 1922 team had opened the road by a remarkably early June 7). Now included in the Kings Hill Scenic Byway, it is the highest pass in Montana to be kept open all winter, providing access to one of the state's oldest ski areas at the summit.

The Prairie Heartland

From King's Hill Pass, Highway 89 cascades down the Little Belts into America's prairie heartland. From the town of Belt to the Canadian border, rolling plains of wheat, barley and native sweetgrass abut the Rocky Mountains, which circle around the Belt Mountains range and meet U.S. 89 north of Great Falls. The short grass prairie ecosystem stretches from the eastern scarp of Montana's Rocky Mountains to the high plains of Oklahoma and Texas. Absent in northern Montana is the gradual transitional zone of foothills typical of other mountain ranges; here, the Rockies jut straight upward out of the grasslands. The northern Rocky Mountain Front preserves some of the grizzly bear's last traditional spring foraging resources on the short grass prairie; Lewis and Clark's journals recount numerous encounters with the ferocious "white bears" during their portage around the Great Falls.

89 Quake dooms Temple of Fun

Two earthquakes shook White Sulphur Springs in the evening of June 25, 1925. The tremblors heavily damaged the 1886 schoolhouse and the new jail. The local auditorium, "The Temple of Fun," was never repaired. However, the townspeople noted one positive outcome: the flow of the hot springs increased by 40 percent.

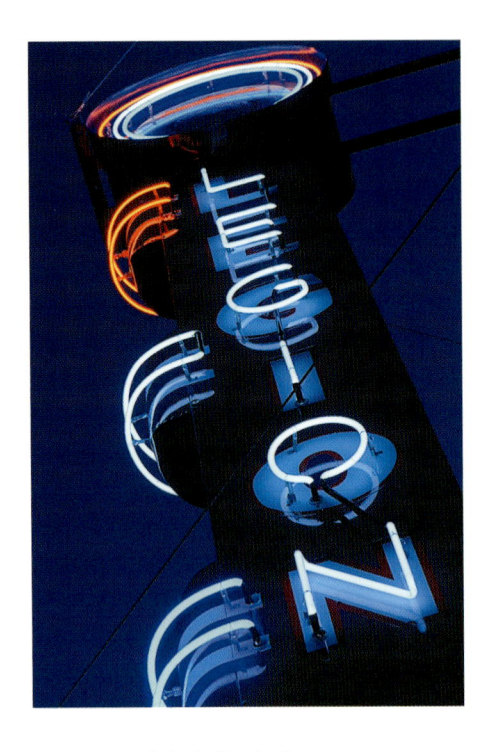

PIG CHASE: Grizzly Day in Dupuyer. (opposite, top left)

SEISMOSAUR: A full-scale skeletal model of the world's largest dinosaur, the Seismosaur, struts above the displays and paleontological laboratory at the Two Medicine Dinosaur Center in Bynum. Nearby, scientists continue excavations at the Egg Mountain site, where dinosaur nests, eggs and babies were discovered. (opposite, top right)

FARM-TO-MARKET: Hutterites, pacifist German-speaking Anabaptists, immigrated to North America beginning in 1873 in search of religious freedom. About 50,000 members live today on communal farms throughout the prairies of Canada and the United States. (opposite, bottom)

LEGION: Recently restored neon sign (above) at the American Legion post in Choteau.

The Corps of Discovery

In the Louisiana Purchase of 1803, France sold to the United States its claim to the full extent of the Mississippi and Missouri Rivers. The next year, President Thomas Jefferson commissioned Meriwether Lewis and William Clark to explore the new territory. Jefferson hoped the Corps of Discovery could find a viable passage across the Rocky Mountains to the Columbia River, establishing both a trade route across the West and a foothold for the country's interests all the way to the Pacific Ocean. Beyond its geographic and scientific inquiries, the mission also was tasked with discovering the northern limits of the Missouri River basin, which defined the border between the United States and Great Britain's Canadian territories.

Scouting reports from natives and French trappers had alerted Lewis and Clark to a great waterfall several hundred miles up the Missouri River. Expecting a cataract similar to Niagara Falls, they discovered instead 15 miles of rapids and cascades. They spent nearly a month scouting, surveying and portaging their supplies and boats around the falls. At the head of the falls, the Corps cached supplies before paddling through the Gates of the Mountains toward the headwaters of the Missouri. Returning the following year, the two captains separated to continue their Montana explorations. Clark took a southerly route that reached the Yellowstone River near Livingston, then built canoes and floated to the Missouri River confluence. Lewis traveled with a small party into Blackfeet country toward the headwaters of the Marias River, reaching within a few miles of the Canadian border that he and Clark helped to establish.

Great Falls: The Electric City

Harnessing the vast power of the Missouri River would have been inconceivable with technology available to Lewis and Clark, when the best waterwheel technology output no more than 10 horsepower. By 1880, however, eastern American cities were powering street lamps with water turbines, and Paris Gibson was inspired by Lewis and Clark's published accounts to see the Great Falls for himself. Gibson, who had built the first commercial flour and woolen mills in Minneapolis, returned to the Great Falls area in 1883 with surveyor Robert Vaughn to plot out a city he envisioned would thrive on the production of hydromechanical and hydroelectric energy.

Black Eagle Dam was completed in 1890 (the fifth and final, Cochrane Dam, was finished in 1958). John D. Ryan, president of Amalgamated Copper Company (later the Anaconda Copper Mining Company), with its extensive mines in Butte, merged several small hydroelectric companies into the Montana Power Company to power both the Milwaukee Road's trains and a copper smelter in Great Falls. Concentrated energy and shipping resources made Great

US Highway 89: Montana ★ 143

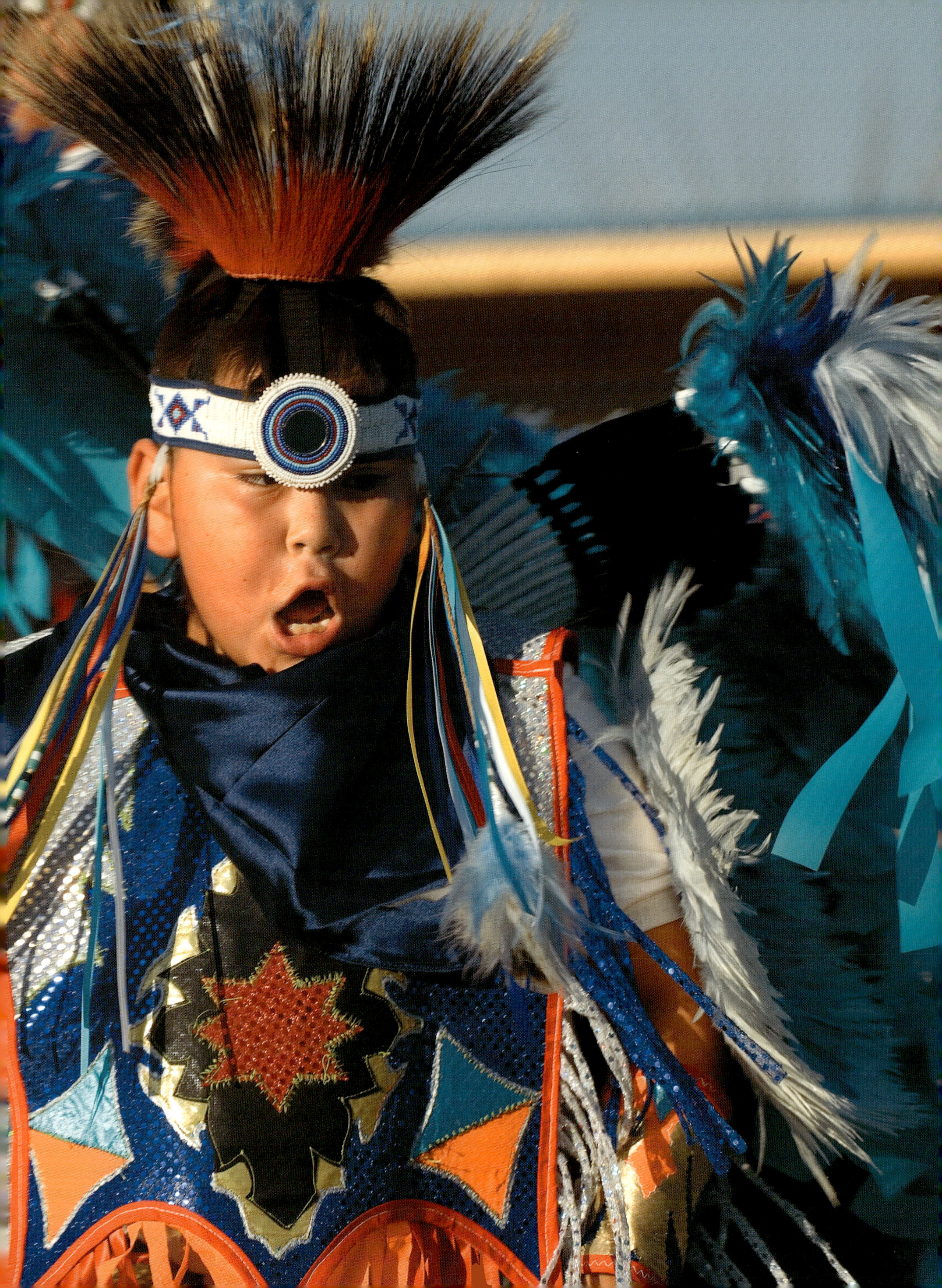

Falls into Montana's second largest city by 1900, despite the fact that the Milwaukee Road reneged on its promise to Gibson to put the city on its main line. Great Falls suffered with the rest of Montana as copper prices declined after World War II, and lost more than 500 jobs in 1980 when the closure of the Anaconda copper mines in Butte idled its smelter. In 1982, 40,000 spectators watched the demolition of the "Big Stack," after last-ditch efforts failed to preserve the town's historic landmark.

From Prairie to Granary
Beneath Montana's Rocky Mountains, Lewis and Clark encountered vast prairies teeming with bison. A century later, the bison had vanished and homesteaders were plowing under native grasses to raise wheat and barley. The Milwaukee Road promoted a program to transport land-hungry homesteaders to Montana, thus, planting the seeds for a steady freight market for dryland-farmed wheat. Other railways advertised similar offers, where special cars delivered families, tools and seeds to contracted agents who carted the homesteaders to their farms, often sight-unseen. Spur lines wove through the Montana grasslands, with grain elevators every few miles piercing the horizon.

The influx of farmers happened to correlate with a series of wet years, but the drought that began in 1917 decimated the homesteaders. By 1922, some estimates suggested that three-quarters of those who had settled in eastern Montana in the unusually wet years of 1909–17 had left the state. Private investors built reservoirs and canals to capture and distribute the winter runoff, then advertised for buyers of irrigated farms "under the ditch." In 1926, Bynum Irrigation District advertisements assured farmers that mortgage payments could be made in crops rather than cash, and noted that native timber for construction was available only 25 miles away.

In the 1930s, relief programs established the Fairfield Bench Farms, relocating eastern Montana farmers to 13,000 acres in Teton County that the federal government had purchased for the resettlement program. Families, many of them German immigrants, received a modest house and outbuildings, and participated in cooperative ventures covering every aspect of rural life, including livestock marketing and even an oil station. Fewer than half of the families, however, completed the purchase on their farms. Many of the drylanders disliked the constraints of irrigated farming, under its strict schedules for opening and closing canal gates. With farms scaled for horse-drawn labor, they struggled to compete against mechanized farms.

The Old North Trail
Some 20 miles distant from the highway, the panorama of the Rocky Mountain Front spans the western skyline north of Fairfield. Between

NORTH AMERICAN INDIAN DAYS: The Blackfeet Nation hosts North American Indian Days in Browning each July. More than half of the enrolled tribal members reside off the reservation; three other, politically separate, bands in Alberta form a confederation with the Montana tribe. Families pitch tipis on the powwow grounds and take part in the four-day celebration of traditional games, dances, drumming and songs. (opposite)

PRAIRIE SKYSCRAPERS: Lodgepoles fill the summer skies (below) during North American Indian Days.

ICEBERG LAKE: The glacier that carved Iceberg Lake (right) no longer exists. Winter ice melts slowly at this high altitude, and hikers can see small icebergs floating on the turquoise surface well into the summer.

MOUNTAIN GOAT: Glacier National Park (opposite, above)

MANY GLACIER HOTEL: Louis Hill adopted a Swiss theme for the Great Northern Railway chain of hotels and chalets in Glacier National Park. (opposite, below)

GRINNELL POINT: Glacier National Park (following pages)

road and ridge line lies evidence of one of humankind's oldest known trails. Long before the Plains Indians acquired horses from Spanish settlements, North American natives had established a braided band of tracks, called the Old North Trail. Estimated to be anywhere from 5,000 to 12,000 years old, it served as a prehistoric migration route from Alaska to Mexico. Later, Plains Indians traveled the Old North Trail with dog- and horse-pulled travois. Métis, a distinct cultural group of mixed European and Indian descent, continued to use it into the 1920s. Méti volunteers are working today on a project to mark the remnants of the trail (now mostly on private property) to commemorate both the trail and their heritage.

Blackfeet Nation
Exalted as horsemen, feared as warriors, the Blackfeet Confederacy at the height of its influence controlled the plains between the

Yellowstone River and modern day Edmonton, Canada. Sometime around 1600, about the time of the first settlements at Jamestown, Virginia, the Blackfeet people began a westward migration from woodlands above the Great Lakes. Once living on the plains, the Blackfeet developed a nomadic culture based on the great bison herds. Bison provided skins for lodges, dried meat to sustain the tribe through bitter cold and blizzards, and delicacies like tongue meat for use in ceremonial dances. Buffalo jumps, areas where bison herds were deliberately stampeded over cliffs, enabled the tribe to stockpile large stores of meat with relative efficiency.

The Blackfeet first encountered horses in a battle against mounted Shoshone around 1730. Less than a generation later, the Blackfeet were respected as the best horsemen of the plains, and their culture had undergone a complete transformation. Horses represented a new kind of wealth, offered greater mobility with their ability to pull heavier travois loads, and extended the range of warfare and raiding parties. By the time Meriwether Lewis encountered them near the Marias River, the Blackfeet had adopted the rifle and had become the dominant people of central Montana and the western Canadian prairie. Of the confederation of four culturally related groups speaking the Blackfeet language, only the Piegans firmly established themselves below the Canadian border.

Neither horse nor rifle protected the Blackfeet against smallpox and the collapse of the bison herds lost to professional hunters that

supplied Eastern markets with buffalo pelts. The 1851 Laramie Treaty (to which the Blackfeet were not a signing party) limited the tribe to hunting north of the Missouri River. Conceding to white settlers' demands for more land, the federal government (without consulting the Blackfeet) constrained the tribe to north of Birch Creek in 1874. Desperate for survival in the aftermath of the disappearance of the buffalo, in 1896 the Blackfeet tribe agreed to sell the western part of the reservation (land now included in Glacier National Park) for $1.5 million dollars.

Highway 89 brought motoring tourists into the heart of the Blackfeet reservation; part of the road-building costs in the 1920s and 1930s were siphoned out of federal Indian affairs budgets. The Blackfeet nation saw little in the way of development until after a disastrous 1964 flood broke three dams along the Rocky Mountain Front and killed 30 people. Today, a hospital and college serve the over 15,000 enrolled tribal members, about half of whom live on the Blackfeet Reservation.

Crown of the Continent

George Bird Grinnell's varied accomplishments reel off like a mini-history of the American West: he served as a naturalist with Lt. Col. George Custer (though not with Custer's disastrous Little Big Horn expedition) and explored Yellowstone soon after it became a national park. In later years, he campaigned to stop poaching of Yellowstone's dwindling bison herd. Grinnell also lived with the Blackfeet tribe and wrote an ethnography of their customs and beliefs. He coined the phrase "Crown of the Continent" to describe the Glacier National Park area in articles he wrote extolling the region's scenery as editor of *Field & Stream*. With Grinnell's advocacy, Glacier National Park was created in 1910.

Glacier National Park straddles the Continental Divide at the U.S.–Canadian border. Its scenery was crafted by massive ice sheets that repeatedly enveloped the northern continent from about two million years ago. About 12,000 years ago, their final retreat revealed the park's intricate forms: cirques, where glaciers carved bowls or basins into mountainsides; aretes, the back-to-back meeting of two cirques; and horn peaks, all that remains of mountains whittled down from all sides. In U-shaped valleys scraped out by rivers of ice, cascades and waterfalls plunge from cliffs into brilliant blue lakes.

This corner of the Rocky Mountains was explored relatively late in American history, in large measure because the Indians who guided military and railway explorers avoided the Blackfeet-controlled Marias Pass, using safer but more difficult mountain routes. James J. Hill, the driving force behind the Great Northern Railway expansion to a transcontinental power, was determined to find the rumored easier route across Montana's northernmost region. In the winter of 1889, the tracks of the "Empire Builder" had reached Havre, Montana. Hill sent his best surveyor to find a route that would avoid expensive tunneling through the Rockies. John F. Stevens (later chief engineer of the Panama Canal) and his Flathead Indian guide Coonsah, stumbled upon the Marias Pass in a snowstorm. Surviving the -40°F night, they managed to return to report their findings, which saved building 100 miles of tracks for the Great Northern's main line.

Passengers on the Great Northern Railway could alight from its East Glacier depot and walk into the national park. Few tourists did so, instead availing themselves of the company's chain of luxurious lodges, linked to remote mountain chalets only by horse trails. Red touring buses transported guests from Great Northern's depots to its lodges on either side of the divide, but until U.S. 2 was completed in 1930, motor vehicles could only cross the park by loading onto a railcar. Private automobiles shipped for $12.50 in 1920, while a passenger paid $1.75.

National Park Service Director Stephen Mather envisioned a highway to connect both sides of the park and he wanted it to showcase the park's scenery, rather than following the more practical route parallel to Great Northern's rails through the Marias pass. The Going-to-the-Sun Road proved to be an

SENTRIES: In 1964 catastrophic dam failures killed 30 people on the Blackfeet reservation, displaced hundreds and inundated Highway 89. Sculptor Jay Laber's family left the Blackfeet reservation. He returned as an artist, turning scrap metal from cars destroyed in the flood into these sentries (above) placed at the northern boundary of the reservation on Highway 89. The sentries face eastward across the prairie to greet the rising sun.

END OF THE ROAD: Piegan port-of-entry station at the end of U.S. 89 (opposite)

engineering feat rivaling the Zion–Mt. Carmel tunnel in Zion National Park. Designed around a key U-turn to preserve the landscape, the highway was carved into the face of the Garden Wall formation, with drops of more than 1,000 feet to the forested valley below. By 1929, tourists could drive to the top of Logan Pass from the west; a long tunnel through Mt. Piegan later opened the eastern approach from Highway 89. The 1933 completion of the Going-to-the-Sun Road had a staggering impact on park attendance: up 50 percent the first year it was open, and from about 22,500 in 1920 to more than 200,000 in 1936. Today, about 3,500 vehicles per day cross the pass during its short summer season.

Mexico to Canada: The Best of the West
From its junction with the Going-to-the-Sun Road at St. Mary village, motorists travel Highway 89's final miles northward to the Canadian border. Just before reaching Babb and the turnoff to the Many Glaciers region of Glacier National Park, Highway 89 passes Triple Divide Mountain, one of the peaks that delineates the park boundary from the Blackfeet reservation. The mountain also separates the Pacific and Missouri River drainages from the Hudson Bay system. Running alongside the Saint Mary River, Highway 89 crosses into its fifth and final continental watershed.

150 ★ The Park-to-Park Highway

Tourists helped fund the construction of the northernmost segment of Highway 89, from Babb to the Canadian border. Horace Albright, attending a 1919 Yellowstone–Glacier Bee-line Association meeting at Glacier National Park, heard from a group of Brooklyn tourists advocating for a better road to connect Glacier to Canada's Waterton Lakes National Park. Albright could only promise a better road when funds became available. At the meeting, the newspaper-sponsored tour group raised $1,000 in 15 minutes and that segment became known as the Brooklyn Eagle Highway.

Highway 89 ends at the lonely Piegan border station. Summer traffic to Waterton Lake turns off U.S. 89 a few miles to the south on the Chief Mountain cutoff, and heavy freight traffic on Interstate 15 crosses the border to the east. The uniformed formality at the Piegan station matches the Nogales entry point, although the U.S.–Canadian border is demarcated by a six-meter strip cleared through the forest, rather than stout fences and heavily armed patrols. A few northbound RVs traveling from Glacier National Park to Canada use the Piegan crossing, along with ranchers pulling stock trailers, Montana Mormons en route to the LDS temple in Cardston, Alberta, and members of the trans-border Blackfeet Indian tribes.

Although the pavement continues northward as Alberta Highway 2, U.S. 89 completes its 1,600-mile journey at Piegan, Montana. From the Sonoran desert, through the Great Basin and across the Rocky Mountains and short-grass prairies, the highway transects landscapes that defined the icons of the American West. From rapidly urbanizing areas to rural corners boasting more cattle than residents, today's Highway 89 motorist encounters the communities and people who are reinventing the Western lifestyle to fit the 21st century.

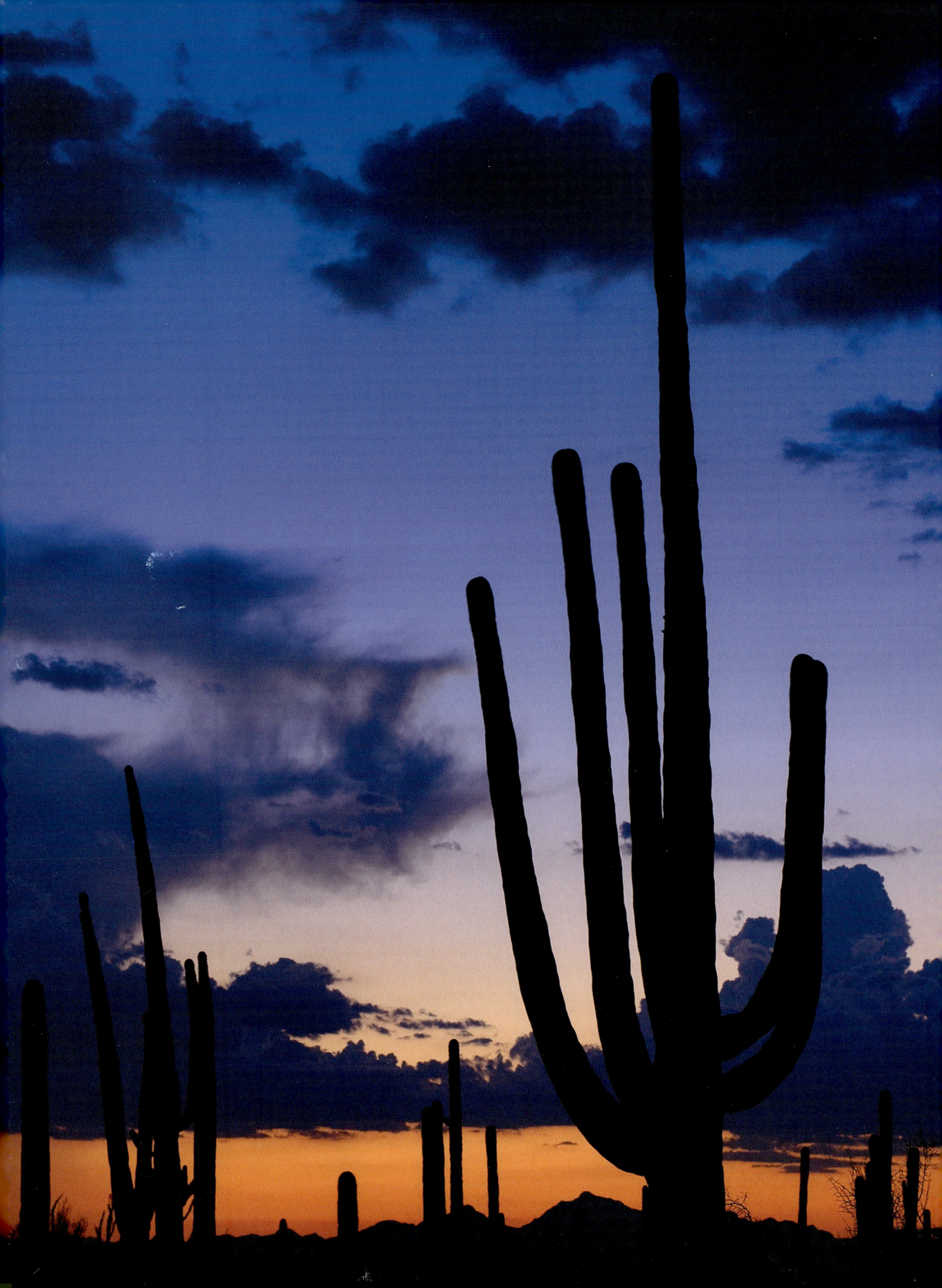

Epilogue
★ ★ ★ The Character of the American West ★ ★ ★ ★ ★ ★ ★

When I began photographing the Highway 89 project, I thought my subject would be the exquisite beauty of its seven national parks. Gradually, as I spent more time on the road, I fell in love with the small towns in between my supposed destinations. I wasn't interested in photographing a nostalgic West that no longer existed; I wanted to show how the people I met were reinventing their Western lifestyles to retain their heritage as change encroached on their communities.

Along the way, I ate ice cream at a church social in Williams, Arizona. A mountain man re-enactor showed me how to throw a tomahawk. A cowboy stampeded a herd of horses at me so I could photograph them at full gallop; afterwards, we discussed how the local National Guard unit's second deployment to the Middle East would impact the families in his small town. My camera gear was pelted with candy tossed from floats in too many parades to count.

As I traveled from state to state, I realized that I made the same picture at the Tucson International Mariachi Conference, at the Mormon Miracle Pageant in Manti, Utah, and at North American Indian Days on the Blackfeet reservation. At first, they just looked like cute kids in different outfits. I found commonality in their parents and grandparents, teaching the next generation "who we are." I saw mothers staggering backstage under stacks of sombreros and dads unloading horse trailers for their aspiring barrel racing daughters. Someone has to judge the 4H rabbit entries in every county fair, and hand down the traditions of a native dance to a worthy grandchild.

The rodeo queen in her cowgirl hat and tiara loping around the arena while talking on her cell phone made me ask: what elements can we alter without undermining the value of our heritage? In the three years I spent documenting this highway, I witnessed so much change: the last ranch that hand-stacked hay in Jackson started using a mechanized baler the year after I made the photograph on

SAGUARO NATIONAL PARK (opposite)

KINGS HILL CABIN: The National Forest Service makes former ranger cabins available to the public for overnight stays at a modest cost. At the Kings Hill Cabin, within a few hundred feet of Highway 89, a young camper added an elaborate entry to the cabin guest book. (above)

OXBOW OF THE SNAKE RIVER: Grand Teton National Park (following pages)

page 116. I made images of a grain elevator, a cousin to the one in Wilsall on page 134, in February 2007; when I returned the following July, it was being dismantled, board-by-board, to be sold as flooring for luxury homes. The national parks may be islands of preservation, but Tucson's subdivisions have pushed to the boundaries of Saguaro National Park.

Not only is the landscape in a precarious state of change: local traditions can disappear, too. Peach Days in Brigham City is still going strong after 105 years, but the Rhubarb Festival in Mt. Pleasant was cancelled. On the other hand, I have come to appreciate that it only takes one or two individuals in a small town to get exciting things done, a leader who provides the catalyst to fill the committee rosters, sell the raffle tickets, line up the local cowboy poet entertainer. An energetic half dozen leaders can make a town sparkle.

In the Intermountain West, where cattle may outnumber residents by the dozen, volunteerism and service keep communities functioning. I met a young officer at the Piegan, Montana, border crossing who wore five hats: customs officer, emergency medical technician, ambulance driver, deputy to the county sheriff and structural firefighter. He explained that the hospital in Browning was so far away that, without volunteers like himself nearby, the "golden hour" could pass without emergency treatment for a traffic accident victim. There simply aren't enough people in north central Montana to do all the jobs that need doing.

I met volunteers who are "defencing" public lands: removing barbed wire to restore wildlife migration corridors around Jackson, Wyoming, an ironic reversal of the idea of progress on the Western range. The spirit of giving brings together some unexpected partners: The Church of Jesus Chris of Latter-day Saints donated funds to build both the traditional Hindu and the Hare Krishna temples along the Wasatch Front.

Some events, like the Hells Angel Prison Run in Florence, Arizona, become so linked to the local

154 ★ Epilogue

FALL FOILAGE: Zion National Park

★ ★ ★ About the Author ★ ★ ★ ★ ★ ★ ★ ★ ★ ★ ★ ★ ★ ★

My favorite photographs record snippets of conversations: between me and another person, the sunrise greeting the landscape, or a mountain goat assessing the danger of my camera. My approach is to be an informed participant, initiating the interchange but letting the conversation unfold naturally. Themes that interest me include the interplay of the human element and landscape; transformations of culture–what we keep, lose, and change; passionate people of any stripe, and the idea of the great American West.

My first road-trip, with my grandparents at age 11, traversed a section of Highway 89. When I moved to Utah in 1993, I began exploring the 10 national parks within a day's drive. I eventually realized that the same highway linked together all of my favorites. After 20 years as an academic administrator, I began documenting this highway full-time, driving over 15,000 miles for the project. My road-trip adventures have become a frequent subject on the blog I have written since 2003.

When not driving America's greatest highway, I live in Salt Lake City with my husband, cats and bountiful garden.

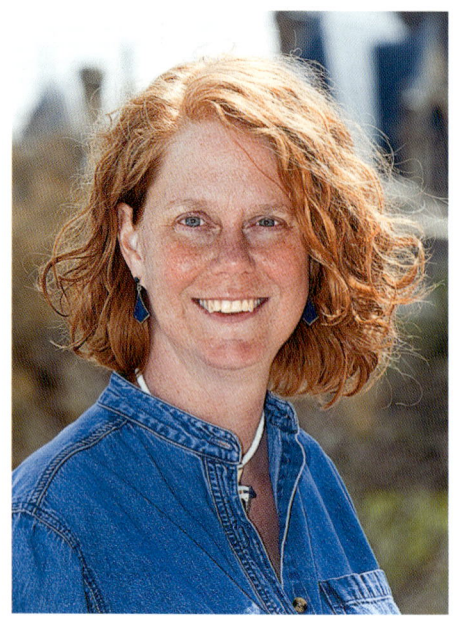

PHOTO: Rich Legg.

★ ★ ★ ★ ★ ★ Highway 89 Online ★ ★ ★ ★ ★ ★

AZ★UT★ID★WY★MT

Fine Art Prints and Gift Items
available online at the US89.com store

- ★ FINE ART PRINTS
- ★ FREE SCREENSAVERS
- ★ POSTERS
- ★ GREETING CARDS
- ★ GIFT ITEMS AND APPAREL

Take a virtual tour of U.S. 89, share your road-trip adventures and meet other Highway 89 enthusiasts at the US89.com website:

- ★ Plan your trip
- ★ Calendar of upcoming events
- ★ Books, maps and more at the US89.com store
- ★ Locals-only insights
- ★ Read up-to-the-minute reviews from readers
- ★ Share with other readers about your travels on Highway 89.
- ★ Adopt a segment of the highway—become an official us89.com blogger and tell the world why your highway is the greatest in the world

Free, fast and fun! Join the U.S. Highway 89 community website today!

www.US89.com